Knowledge Management in Education

Knowledge Management in Education

Enhancing Learning & Education

Edward Sallis | Gary Jones

KOGAN
PAGE

First published in 2002

Kogan Page Limited
120 Pentonville Road
London N1 9JN
UK

Stylus Publishing Inc
22883 Quicksilver Drive
Sterling VA 20166-2012
USA

British Library Cataloguing in Publication Data

A CIP record for this book is available from the British Library.

ISBN 0 7494 3495 3

Typeset by JS Typesetting, Wellingborough, Northants
Printed and bound in Great Britain by Biddles Ltd, Guildford and King's Lynn
www.biddles.co.uk

Contents

v

The authors

Dr Edward Sallis is a well-known educationalist with 30 years' experience in further and higher education in the UK and Jersey. He is Principal and Chief Executive of Highlands College, the further, adult and higher education college of the States of Jersey in the British Channel Islands. A specialist in organizational development and strategy, Dr Sallis holds degrees from London, Newcastle and Brunel University. He is a Fellow of the Institute of Management and a Chartered Marketer and gained his PhD from the Bristol Business School of the University of the West of England.

His numerous publications include *The Machinery of Government (1982)*; *People in Organisations (1989)*, which he co-wrote with his wife Kate Sallis; *Total Quality Management (1992)*, co-authored with Dr Peter Hingley, and *Total Quality Management in Education*, the third edition of which will be published by Kogan Page in 2002. He writes regularly for the Channel Islands business magazine *Business Brief* as well as for national journals, and has taken part in many national and international educational initiatives in the fields of quality assurance, organizational development, lifelong learning and knowledge management.

Dr Sallis is a member of the British Irish Council's sectoral working group on the knowledge economy, for which Jersey is the lead jurisdiction. He is the director of the BIC's 'Bridging the Digital Divide' research project, which is being run in collaboration with the governments of Eire, the UK, Northern Ireland, Wales, Scotland, Guernsey, Jersey and the Isle of Man. He is also a member of the Association of Colleges' National Policy Forum.

Dr Gary Jones is the Deputy Principal at Highlands College, Jersey, where he is responsible for the curriculum, quality assurance and the development of information technology. An Associate of the Chartered Institute of Bankers, he has considerable experience of teaching business and social studies in sixth form colleges, and further and higher education in the UK and Jersey.

The authors

He holds a first degree in Economics and International Relations from the University of Wales and a masters degree and a doctorate in Education from Bristol University. He regularly gives papers to educational research conferences on topics related to knowledge management. He is involved in a number of research and consultancy projects, most recently an e-learning project for the East Sussex Learning and Skills Council. He has directed a range of ICT action research projects in conjunction with Professor Bridget Somekh of Manchester Metropolitan University.

Dr Jones was formerly Highlands College's Director of the Digital Curriculum and was responsible for much of the college's successful and innovative ICT development, and for promoting knowledge management. He has extensive experience of using ICT as a tool in education and training and has played a major role within Jersey Education Service's major initiative to use ICT to transform learning.

In October 2000, Dr Jones was awarded the National Information and Learning Technology Association (NILTA) National ICT Leadership Award for his innovative approach to motivating staff at Highlands College to use ICT to promote student learning.

Acknowledgements

We wish to thank many people for their help in writing this book. Like all such endeavours, it was a collaborative effort. Our knowledge has been gained from many sources, and in paying tribute to our influences there is a risk of overlooking individuals who have assisted us.

Particular thanks go to States of Jersey IT/IS Advisor Peter Griffiths, for making us a part of his vision for e-business in Jersey, and to Tom McKeon, Jersey's Director of Education, who made possible Jersey's innovative strategy relating to ICT in education. Our Chairman of Governors, Deputy Gerald Voisin, has been a great help in all manner of ways and has been a great source of inspiration.

We would also like to give a special thank you to Professor Bridget Somekh of Manchester Metropolitan University, and to Dr Terry Melia CBE, Chair of the Learning and Skills Development Agency, and former Chief Inspector of the Further Education Funding Council for England. Terry has been an enormous influence on our thinking about educational issues and has provided much practical assistance to Highlands College in developing its own approaches to knowledge management. Without him, our thinking would have much impoverished.

Our colleagues at Highlands College, Jersey, deserve a special thank you for helping us in so many different ways. Our great friend Brian Woods, Director of Resources, planned the physical implementation of Highlands' knowledge strategy. He has always kept us on our toes, and constantly and productively challenged our thinking and provided us with new ideas and insights, particularly on how to manage processes and people. We would also like to thank the academic and support staff of Highlands College for creating the conditions in which we were allowed to try out new ideas.

Finally, we would like to thank Kate Sallis and Serafina Jones. They have helped us throughout the writing of this book and without their support it would never have been completed.

Introduction: the knowledge age

'In an economy where the only certainty is uncertainty, the one sure source of lasting competitive advantage is knowledge.' (Ikujiro Nonaka, 1991)

Practical knowledge-related studies have enjoyed an upsurge of interest in recent years, and *knowledge management* and the *knowledge economy* have been generally recognized as important fields of intellectual pursuit since the early 1990s. At about this time, economists and policy-makers started writing about certain changes taking place in the economy and in society. They described a 'new, knowledge-driven economy', and identified the need for all of us to recognize that we were now living in the 'knowledge age'.

Ten years ago, who would have predicted that the market capitalization of companies such as Microsoft and Cisco Systems would be greater than those of the big oil companies or the giants of the motor industry? (And this despite the difficult time technology stocks have had on stock exchanges since the year 2000.) Indeed, 10 years ago, very few people would have even heard of Cisco Systems! Who could have foreseen the reality of tele-medicine or e-commerce? Who in higher education would have imagined that it would be possible to achieve a globally accredited degree delivered via the Internet?

In our modern world, rapid and unpredictable change happens as a result of the explosive developments in the global economy linked to new telecommunications, multimedia and IT possibilities. These technologies allow a linking of the formerly divergent technologies of telecommunications, television and computing. In this climate of change, many traditional economic ideas appear less and less relevant, yet there is no consensus about how best to replace them. New and radical thinking is needed on the nature of employment and the way our organizations – public, voluntary and private – are managed and organized.

The importance of knowledge

The issues of the knowledge age are global ones, but the advances in technology make it increasingly difficult to predict what the world will be like in the next five years, let alone the next 10 or 20. According to Microsoft founder Bill Gates, predictors tend to *over*estimate changes that might happen in three years time, but *under*estimate the changes that might have occurred 10 years on. This uncertainty gives knowledge a prime importance. If the external environment is uncertain, organizations have to fall back on their own resources – knowledge and their pool of intellectual capital. Their knowledge base is perhaps the only certainty that most organizations have. The World Bank's 1998 Development Report drives home the point:

> *The international trend affects economies at all levels of development. For countries in the vanguard of the world economy the balance between knowledge and resources has shifted so far towards the former that knowledge has become perhaps the most important factor determining the standard of living. . . . Today's most technologically advanced economies are truly knowledge-based. (World Bank, 1998)*

The knowledge age is prefaced on the sheer volume of information that is being generated today, and on the accessibility of that information. The quantity of the information is increasing at a staggering rate, in part due to the sheer amount of computing power available, in part to the general explosion of knowledge and research. Developments in computing power have been astonishing – today's modern luxury cars have more of it than Apollo 11 did – and that power is used largely by businesses and consumers to search for knowledge, particularly via the World Wide Web. It has been estimated that there are over 8 million unique Web sites worldwide and that the current rate of growth is about 50 per cent per annum. About 2.5 billion documents are directly accessible and this figure is growing at a rate of some 7 million pages per day. If you combine the public Web with all the company Web sites, government databases and Intranet sites, there may be as many as 550 billion documents existing in a digital networked format around the world. Computing power and accessibility to information is making the world aware of the potential of using and creating knowledge.

For decades, Peter Drucker has been telling us that more and more work is becoming knowledge-based. In *Post Capitalist Society* he wrote, 'The basic economic resource is no longer capital, nor natural resources, nor labour. It is and will be knowledge. Value is now created by "productivity" and "innovation", both applications of knowledge to work.' (Drucker, 1993.)

When the ground-breaking 1944 Education Act was passed in the UK, only a minority of work could have been described as knowledge work. Around 20 per cent of those in employment were in white collar or professional occupations and the rest of the workforce was employed in manual work – labourers, factory workers, miners, steelworkers, construction workers, or shipbuilders. The situation is now the reverse, and there is a diminishing need for unskilled and semi-skilled workers. Instead, our economies require people with high-level managerial, technical and knowledge-based skills and a graduate education. Today's employees are no longer directed and controlled by Taylorist automata; they are much more likely to be autonomous and creative knowledge workers. Increasingly, employers expect their workforce to be educated, creative and enterprising, and to possess a wide range of key skills. This has profound implications both for education and business, dictating our present and future educational and organizational priorities.

Over the past half-century, the world's major economies have evolved from a reliance on manufacturing industries to those based on intellectual and creative skills. In a world increasingly dominated by global communications and mass knowledge cultures, the possession and use of intellectual capital is becoming the key organizational resource. The success of the new business giants is not based on their command of raw materials or physical capital. They prosper instead on the exploitation of new ideas and on new forms of innovation. The creativity of a company is more important than its productivity ability or even its technical ability. Recently, the Swedish firm Ericsson took over domination of the mobile phone market from former leader Motorola, and was itself leapfrogged by Finland's Nokia. This was partly because Nokia had the capacity to innovate faster and to understand the needs of customer better. Companies such as Microsoft, Nokia and Cisco Systems are economic giants because they use knowledge as the basic tool of their business.

The UK's Department of Trade and Industry wrote the following in its report 'Our Competitive Future: Building the Knowledge-Driven Economy':

A knowledge-driven economy is one in which the generation and exploitation of knowledge has come to play the predominant part in the creation of wealth. It is not simply about pushing back the frontiers of knowledge; it is also about the more effective use and exploitation of all types of knowledge in all manner of economic activity. (Department of Trade and Industry, 2000)

Why knowledge management?

The notion of knowledge management is both a theoretical and practical response to the needs of the knowledge age and the explosion in information. It is about the realization that knowledge is the key driver behind organizational success. The workplace of the early 21st century is very different from that of only a decade or so ago. It will change rapidly in the future and in directions that are unpredictable. The only certainty will be change. Modern organizational life rests on the following foundations:

▮ the need to respond rapidly to new economic ideas and business models;
▮ an ever-increasing rate of technological change;
▮ rapid innovation in products and services, with products and services having a greater and greater knowledge content;
▮ markets that are becoming global and increasingly competitive;
▮ the challenge of leadership and management issues, which are becoming increasingly complex and problematic;
▮ a speed of change that means that organizations are increasingly susceptible to the obsolescence of their knowledge base;
▮ the need for lifelong learning, knowledge creation and sharing among workforces;
▮ stakeholders that are increasingly sophisticated and demanding.

The aims of this book

Knowledge Management in Education is a sister publication to *Total Quality Management in Education* (third edition published by Kogan Page in 2002). Both books examine important management ideas that are well established in leading corporate cultures, and explain their utility in the educational setting.

This book focuses on the impact that effective management of knowledge can have on organizations and looks at some of the practical knowledge strategies that can be employed by educational establishments. While knowledge management is a growing field, very little has been written about it in the educational context. The authoritative *The Knowledge Management Yearbook 2000–2001* (ed. James W. Cortanda and John A. Woods) has a definitive bibliography of current knowledge management writings, but very few of them have any direct educational relevance. This is surprising, considering that education is about the creation and application of knowledge. After all, the business of education is knowledge.

Education may have failed to fully appreciate the potential of knowledge management, but it is not alien to it. There may be some scepticism in education circles that business ideas can relate directly to educational practice, but this is misguided. Knowledge management is, in fact, in tune with the culture of education and education should be leading the way in making knowledge management a key part of its culture. Currently, it is not making the grade, but there are many signs that this is about to change. Now that league tables, inspection, performance management and academic audit are the order of the day, it is important to realize that sharing and harvesting knowledge can have considerable benefits. It can contribute to better management of the challenges of greater accountability, as well as providing new ideas for the future. Education should be the natural home of the discipline. It is our thesis that the underlying principles of knowledge management are as applicable to education as to any other organization, and that other institutions may have much to learn from the practice of the educational sector.

Knowledge Management in Education has been written to give managers and staff working in education an insight into the world of knowledge management, and to provide them with practical tools so that they can adapt their own management processes to meet the challenges of the knowledge age. Knowledge management has been put forward as a major survival strategy for organizations. It is more than that; it is a means of strengthening their performance. Understanding how knowledge is created and managed is as essential for education as for any other type of organization. Just as businesses can improve the efficiency and effectiveness of their organizations through sound knowledge management, so educational institutions can realize the potential of knowledge creation and the power of knowledge-sharing in order to enhance the learning of pupils, students and staff.

1 What is knowledge management?

'Knowledge is our most important engine of production.'

Alfred Marshall, Economist

This chapter explores the dimensions of knowledge management and the key concepts that underpin it. It looks at why knowledge is so important to 21st-century organizations and asks why there is a need for an emerging knowledge discipline. It investigates the nature of knowledge and identifies the two important concepts, namely explicit and tacit knowledge, which are crucial to understanding knowledge management and which form the basis for managing organizational knowledge. It concludes with some of the implications that knowledge management insights can have for educational institutions.

Knowledge – the 21st-century resource

Knowledge is the key resource of the information age. Today, the importance of managing knowledge and know-how is a categorical organizational imperative. Without understanding their own process for knowledge creation, organizations are unlikely to continue as functioning enterprises. The successful 21st-century organizations – schools, small businesses or corporate giants – will be those that make the best use of their information and knowledge and use them to create sustained additional value for their stakeholders.

While the power of knowledge has always been seen as important (witness the role of the spy), businesses and public bodies today make use of knowledge in a very different manner. The emphasis is shifting from secrecy to sharing. Where once knowledge was scarce, and hoarded as a source of power and influence, today the power of knowledge is in its communication and in its use as a positive, creative force. Where once knowledge was the province of the few – the rich and the powerful – today, the power of the Internet means that vast amounts of knowledge are potentially the province of everyone.

The problem today is not how to *find* information, but how to *manage* it. We have moved from the age of secrecy to the age of information overload. The challenge for organizations is how to process knowledge, sorting out what is important from what is not, and use the best of it creatively. If an organization does not or cannot learn from its own store of knowledge it stands little chance of survival. Making the best use of its own knowledge makes an organization successful.

Knowledge-based organizations are the likely winners in the new economic order. They are the ones with all or most of the following characteristics:

■ they recognize knowledge as the main driver of their success;
■ they have a clearly formulated vision for knowledge creation;
■ their values emphasize their commitment to managing knowledge;
■ they have a widespread enthusiasm and commitment for knowledge creation;
■ their employees are valued for their intellect and their capacity to create new knowledge;
■ they have high levels of individual, team and organizational learning;
■ they use ICT and other new technologies in creative ways;
■ their organizational culture facilitates knowledge creation;
■ their organizational culture supports the development and testing of prototypes.

Origins of knowledge management

Knowledge is a vastly intriguing and important subject. Knowledge is at the heart of civilization, underlying all that we think, believe and do, and questions about its nature are as old as civilization itself. Knowledge has brought our technologies into being and has transformed our world. Knowing and understanding things and being creative are the basis of our learning, as well as our political, educational and business life.

And yet, while knowledge as a discipline is as old as recorded history, knowledge *management* is a relatively new discipline. It has come to prominence because of the sheer volume of the information available in the modern world. As a major discipline it is barely a decade old, and yet its roots can be found in philosophy and psychology, as well as business and management theory. Its intellectual origins can be traced back to the industrial revolutions of the 18th and 19th centuries and to the management thinking that accompanied the rise of mass production and large-scale manufacturing. Knowledge management has its origins in the need for companies to harness the scientific, human and intellectual capital at their disposal. Its emergence as a separate discipline can be attributed to the change from managing muscles to managing brains, and to the vast growth of knowledge caused by the combined technologies of the computer, scientific research, telecommunications, digital television and the Internet.

Knowledge management is still in its infancy, and there is a considerable element of novelty about it. Nevertheless, interest in it is expanding at an enormous rate. Until comparatively recently, the term 'knowledge management' had a comparatively narrow definition. When first used in the 1980s it was limited to describing artificial intelligence and the processes associated with the application of computing. By the time it started to be used in management literature, in the early 1990s, it had taken on a broader perspective, although with little real consensus about its meaning. This is still the case to a certain extent, although there is now far more clarity and focus over its meaning.

The term 'knowledge management' is used to describe everything from the application of new technology to the broader endeavour of harnessing the intellectual capital of an organization. Nevertheless, a consensus is developing around the idea of knowledge management as being about *learning to know what we know*. This perspective is the one that is explored in this book. The idea is that knowing what we know, and using it creatively and productively, is the major source of economic value and competitive advantage at the disposal of any organization.

However, we need to remember that one aspect of *knowing what we know* is not always that simple. There is much knowledge that an organization is not conscious of and, in addition, organizations need to have a process to *know what they do not know but should know*. The latter is difficult but important. Identifying what an organization should know requires insight and vision. Scenario planning (*see* Chapter 5) is one important technique that helps us to understand futures and alternatives, and brings to light what an organization needs to know.

Different types of knowledge

In the world of knowledge management, successful organizations are those that realize the importance of making the most of what they know, and at the same time develop new value by creating knowledge. Every organization has an enormous amount of information at its disposal – about its economic environment, and its products, services, processes, technologies, customers, clients, suppliers and competitors. It can all be used to the organization's advantage, but utilizing that knowledge is not a simple matter. Knowledge is after all not a tangible product, or a material thing like land, labour and physical capital. Neither is it all of a kind. Some knowledge is very easy to access and cheap to harness, while other knowledge is locked away in people's minds and harder to use effectively. An organization may not even be aware that it has some kinds of knowledge – this may become clear only when key individuals leave or when a competitor highlights it. Where the knowledge base forms the essential capability of the organization, this type of knowledge may be called *critical knowledge*.

Some knowledge is deeply embedded in an organization. *Embedded knowledge* is the technical or intellectual core of the organization's activities. In education it is the essential subject knowledge of the educators; in a marketing company it may be its client database; in an engineering company it may be the patents than govern its technical processes. The challenge for knowledge management is to make better use of all organizational knowledge, and to find appropriate means and technologies to make sense and use of the knowledge embedded in the staff of an organization, and what lies behind that organization's processes.

Knowledge is not static. It is ever-changing and what was once essential and embedded can quickly become out-dated and obsolete. Strengths can quickly turn into weaknesses, because of technological change or the turbulence of markets. Successful knowledge organizations are those, like 3M, which are always encouraging new ideas and new products, and which encourage the growth of new knowledge. *Creative knowledge* is the key to future success.

Knowledge management is not a magic cure

Despite the undisputed importance of knowledge in the modern world, not everyone regards the subject of knowledge management favourably. Some commentators dismiss it as just another management fashion, one of many in recent years. Some might see it, wrongly, as a cure-all for every business performance problem. In the past, total quality management was seized upon by many as the Holy Grail of business change, capable of solving most organizational problems and of delivering continuous outstanding business performance. When it did not deliver everything that was claimed for it, many commentators consigned TQM to the dustbin of management theory.

Management ideas such as knowledge management should not be seen in this way. They are not magic cures. Organizational performance is not like that. Instead, they should be seen as offering an important insight into the organizational condition. Undoubtedly, the notion that an organization should nurture, share and exploit its knowledge assets is an important and original insight. In retrospect it is clear that the intelligent exploitation of organizational knowledge has always had a major impact on the fortunes of businesses, and has always been a critical success factor for any organization. All organizations use and generate knowledge. Some, like educational establishments, have knowledge at their core. In the course of their daily existence they process information and turn it into knowledge. They then use that knowledge and, by combining it with their values, strategies and experiences, make decisions based on it. Knowledge management has to be integrated into everything that an organization does. As such, it is a necessary, although not a sufficient condition, for long-term organizational success.

The importance of harnessing knowledge

Despite recognition of the need to manage knowledge resources properly, the understanding of how to go about doing it properly is still in its infancy. Many organizations are at a loss to know how best to achieve it. And in some sectors, such as education, there have been few attempts at taking it on. Most organizational leaders know that their organization's knowledge resides in the head of their employees, but they do not know how to unlock it. If this is the case, it is particularly serious when key individuals leave the organization. If there are no mechanisms for capturing their knowledge, it goes out of the door with them. Knowledge loss can be immensely damaging. It has been estimated that the average business loses half of its stock of knowledge every five years from employee turnover.

Ignoring the need to properly harness corporate and individual knowledge may result in a number of unfortunate consequences, including some of the following:

▌ loss of expertise and knowledge;
▌ loss of income and revenue;
▌ losses in productivity;
▌ lost or missed opportunities;
▌ having to reinvent the wheel;
▌ loss of knowledge of best practices;
▌ loss of learning opportunities;
▌ damage to key customer, supplier and stakeholder relationships;
▌ reductions in the quality of future knowledge;
▌ damage to the organization's culture and social capital;
▌ other organizations capitalizing on ideas that were once their own.

Formal and informal knowledge

In all organizations there is a huge amount of information and data available, coming from a multitude of sources, in all sorts of forms. It may originate from the organization's staff, from its business partners, customers or suppliers, and from a range of other sources, including online databases, trade catalogues and magazines, product manuals, trade fairs, exhibitions, conferences and seminars, external consultancy, university research departments. It may also take the form of intelligence about competitors.

Formal knowledge comes in a wide range of formats – official policy documents, scribbled notes, reports, e-mails, correspondence files, Web pages, notes of telephone conversations, letters, memos, quality manuals, financial records, staff handbooks, computer printouts, minutes of meetings, telephone directories and database records. It can be the result of the work of individuals, committees, teams, project groups, working parties and focus groups. Some organizational knowledge is very difficult to record and store, while some is readily processed. Some is regarded as valuable and will be carefully recorded, filed, archived and stored, and is protected by data protection legislation. However, the bulk of our formal knowledge is regarded as having little lasting value or utility. It is shredded, disregarded, forgotten, lost or just thrown away. What constitutes useful, valuable or important knowledge depends on the values and aims of the organization and the priorities it establishes; of course, organizations can get it wrong and dispose of knowledge that turns out to be valuable.

As a corporate asset, knowledge can be the defining feature of the strategy of any organization and gives it its distinctiveness. Knowledge provides the collective memory and the intellectual property of the organization. Brands, logos and patents are examples of intellectual property in an organization. Often, the brand is more critical for success than the product or service, because it is the brand of which the consumer has most know-ledge. When an organization seeks to become a centre of excellence, a market leader, a brand leader, and world class, it is seeking to develop and exploit its knowledge assets for competitive advantage. Its exploitation of formal knowledge can give it the lead.

As well as the organization's formal knowledge, there is also the folklore of the organization, known as *informal knowledge*. It can be just as valuable a source of information, and although it is an intangible it must not be overlooked. It is the knowledge about how things *really* work and what *really* keeps things going. Informal knowledge relates to the difference between the way things are and the way they should be; the difference between the world as it is seen and the official definition. In every organiza-tion there will be a number of people who can tell the *real* story.

The communication of informal organizational knowledge is the modern form of the ancient art of storytelling, with tales and legends being passed on through various media. The informal grapevine can involve gossip, conversation, chats in the corridor or by the water fountain. It can be via telephone or, increasingly, via e-mail, text messaging or online chat. All these means keep the folklore of the organization alive. It is rarely written down, and almost never officially documented or archived. Such stories have been for a long time a major source for popular journalism but other organizations have been slow to recognize the importance of folklore.

Gossip can be very accurate and perceptive, but it may also be misleading, incorrect, wrong, malicious, and out of date. It is very difficult to replace it with more timely and accurate information, and is often considered to be *true* even if there is official information to the contrary. Many people, especially in the lower echelons of an organization, prefer to believe informal knowledge rather than the official version; managers disregard it at their peril. Informal knowledge is socially constructed and is kept alive by its constant repeating. When it has lost its usefulness it fades away and dies, and yet much of it has enormous staying power. The message is often in the telling and it plays a crucial role in defining the culture of the organization.

One key to successful knowledge management is the exploitation of all forms of knowledge, both formal and informal. This can be achieved by developing open, knowledge-sharing cultures and processes, linked to appropriate technologies. However, organizations need to be clear that knowledge is more than information. Simply having more and better information does not mean that we are any more knowledgeable. In fact, the opposite may often be the case. Information by itself can lead to confu-sion, and information overload is one of today's most serious problems, both for individuals and organizations. It is the *productive use* of information that is important. Knowledge is information that has been consciously processed, and has established meaning and value to those who use it.

Formal and informal knowledge

▌ Formal knowledge is that contained in official documentation.
▌ Formal knowledge is usually stored, filed and catalogued.
▌ Formal knowledge can provide distinctiveness and market branding.
▌ Informal knowledge is the folklore of the organization.
▌ Informal knowledge is usually transmitted by word of mouth.
▌ Informal knowledge is a powerful means of transmitting ideas.
▌ Many employees believe the folklore rather than official explanations.
▌ The key to organizational success is to exploit both formal and informal knowledge.

What is knowledge?

Knowledge is at the heart of human civilization. It is the engine of creativity and culture and defines our humanity. As a consequence, knowledge represents a great deal more than information, with which it is commonly confused. Knowledge is information in use, and it is the interaction of information with the human mind that gives it meaning and purpose.

Epistemology, the philosophical study that examines the nature, sources and the limits of knowledge, is beyond the scope of this book. This book does not aim to answer questions about *how* we know what we know, and the difference between belief and knowledge. Nevertheless, certain philosophical as well as psychological insights can help distinguish information from knowledge, and help us to understand the role that knowledge plays in the organizational context.

One crucial difference between information and knowledge is that knowledge requires a *knowing subject*. There is a sense of commitment to knowledge that is lacking in relation to information. Information can only become knowledge when people apply their intellect to it, and interpret it. Information becomes knowledge when it is believed, understood and applied. Without that intervention of the human mind, data and information are merely artefacts. Information only becomes knowledge if someone *knowledgeable* gives it meaning. A knowledgeable person uses his or her intellect to make sense of information and, from it, develops new thinking, ideas and concepts and makes them work in new, creative and innovative ways.

Knowledge is an integral part of the complex learning processes of all human beings. This view of knowledge is important because it helps to emphasize that knowledge involves activity, thought and learning. As Davenport and Prusak have said, 'Knowledge derives from minds at work' (1998). Knowledge creation is a conscious process and one that changes the world in which we live. For this reason, the effects of acquiring and using knowledge can be seen in the difference they make to the way things are done. This is the point about knowledge management. It is about the success that can come from using knowledge in smarter and better ways. Managing knowledge is about improvement, innovation and achieving objectives; crucially, it involves learning.

At this point, it is worth making another distinction, this time between *knowledge for understanding* and *knowledge for action*. While it is important to have knowledge to help us understand and explain the world (knowledge for understanding), in an organizational context what is most important is using the understanding gained to create ideas that can be used to improve or to create new products and services (knowledge for action). Practical managers are interested in those ideas that can change the way people think and behave, and can ensure the future survival of the organization. Knowledge management is based primarily on the concept of knowledge for action.

Knowledge is a difficult and a slippery concept, and it is not easy to provide a simple all-purpose definition. It takes different forms and different commentators have their own interpretation of it. However, it may be useful to attempt a working definition, otherwise knowledge management may be confused with data-processing or information-handling, and may come to be regarded as solely a technical process. Knowledge management is not a set of technical solutions to a problem, but a human and social process (which may be facilitated by technological solutions).

A definition can also provide an opportunity for concise reflection. Our definition has been devised for organizations needing to manage their knowledge:

Knowledge is a key organizational asset that creates and adds value to the organization's products and services. It is composed of those insights and understandings that give meaning to the information and data at the organization's disposal. Knowledge originates in the minds of knowing subjects, who evaluate and interpret it in the light of the framework provided by their experiences, values, culture and learning. In the organizational context, knowledge takes a range of explicit forms and formats, including processes, procedures and documents, as well as more tacit forms, including values, beliefs, emotions, judgements and prejudices. If properly applied, all forms of knowledge can provide the driving force for action.

Knowledge is:

∎ more than information;
∎ social;
∎ the key organizational asset;
∎ constructed in the mind of a knowing subject;
∎ active understanding;
∎ dependent on individual perspective;
∎ an integral element in learning;
∎ a key organizational asset;
∎ the spur to action;
∎ both explicit and tacit.

Two concepts of knowledge

Knowledge is slippery, complex and multi-dimensional. In order to manage it best, we need to understand some of the complexities surrounding it. Making a distinction between two different but important types of knowledge is crucial to knowledge management, and to using knowledge effectively in the organizational context.

The two types of knowledge are generally known as *explicit* and *tacit*. In order to harvest the different types successfully, different strategies are required. Of the two concepts, explicit knowledge is what most people think of when the term 'knowledge' is used. This is because explicit knowledge is easier to understand than tacit knowledge, and easier to manage and manipulate. Explicit knowledge is precise and codifiable, while tacit knowledge is more intangible and personal.

Explicit knowledge

As the management of explicit knowledge is often seen as a technical issue, knowledge-management literature tends to use industrial and technological metaphors to describe the relevant activities. Many organizations employ the language of physical exploitation, with analogies from mining or prospecting – 'mining', 'drilling down' or 'digging' for information. These industrial analogies are often complemented by a range of distributive metaphors, which describe how knowledge is classified and made available within the organization. Knowledge is 'stored', 'captured', 'packaged', 'husbanded', 'warehoused' or 'distributed'. The value of the knowledge is established using financially-derived metaphors such as 'intellectual capital' and 'knowledge assets', and knowledge is described as being 'levered' when its value is exploited for profit.

These metaphors treat explicit knowledge as a commodity like any other factor of production. While it is possible to treat some knowledge in this way, the metaphors are inappropriate for all kinds of knowledge. Much of an organization's tacit knowledge does not fit the pattern. It is extremely difficult to drill, lever or mine the less tangible and personal types of knowledge.

Unfortunately, some of the knowledge-management literature also uses the term 'knowledge' as if it were all of a type, a universal software programme that takes care of all of the organization's activities. The problem with seeing knowledge in this way is that it tends to classify all knowledge as a thing or an artefact, something that can be easily managed and manipulated for the organization's benefit. This can be misleading and can cause problems because it confuses the two concepts of knowledge. Much knowledge is best thought of as a process rather than a thing. If we recognize this, knowledge management takes on two distinct but complementary roles. The first is about organizing and classifying explicit knowledge, whereas the second is the study of how people communicate and interact in organizations. In this second role, knowledge management becomes aligned to the study of organizational culture.

Because explicit knowledge is the knowledge that can be most easily articulated and transmitted, it is sometimes called *codified* or *declarative* knowledge; the terms may also be used to describe formal knowledge. It has its source in formal organizational documentation such as procedure manuals, mathematical equations, patents, procedures, technical reports, computer databases, files, library books, archived documents, letters, organizational policies and financial statements. Educational establishments routinely collect huge amounts of this kind of information in the form of data about students, their background, their progress, their assessments and their examination results.

Harvesting formal and explicit knowledge is essential for the proper functioning of an organization. However, it is usually just collected for the task in hand. Thought is rarely given as to how it can be exploited for the organization's long-term benefit, even though the potential power of harnessing it can be enormous. Explicit knowledge can be shared and used to create new and useful knowledge. After all, it is easy to communicate and can be transferred relatively easily between individuals, both within and outside the organization. For example, because of modern technology, it can be downloaded into databases and made accessible over company Intranets and the Internet.

Using explicit knowledge effectively is one of the challenges of knowledge management. It is often a difficult and time-consuming task to find and locate particular pieces of information, in a form that is readily accessible. While an organization's store of explicit knowledge should support proper decision making, in most cases organizational hurdles limit employees' ability to gain the maximum value from it. This is particularly true when information exists in a multitude of locations and formats, so that it is not always apparent where to find it. Frequently there is no way of knowing, for example, whether a particular piece of information is out of date. In many educational institutions, producing the school or college's organization chart, programme self-evaluation, student recruitment figures, the internal telephone directory, or a list of course and programmes, should be a quick and routine activity, but it is often a time-consuming chore. Apparently, finding the internal telephone extension list takes at least five minutes in the average organization.

Explicit or declarative knowledge:

■ is about 'knowing that' (declarative knowledge) (*see* page 11);
■ is objective and formal knowledge;
■ is tangible information;
■ is capable of being codified;
■ is consciously accessible;
■ can be easy networked on databases and Intranets;
■ can be easily communicated and transferred to others by letters, e-mail, the Internet and so on.

Tacit knowledge

The two types of knowledge, explicit and tacit, are complementary. Tacit knowledge is at the very heart of the knowledge-management process, and understanding its many facets is essential to an understanding of the subject.

The concept of tacit knowledge derives from the works of the philosopher Michael Polanyi, who wrote *The Tacit Dimension* in 1966 and a second study *Personal Knowledge* in 1973. Tacit knowledge is significantly different from the formal and objective explicit knowledge. Polanyi sums up the concept in his memorable phrase, 'We know much more than we can tell'. In using this phrase he illustrates how difficult tacit knowledge is to communicate and to share. The term 'tacit knowledge' highlights the importance of a subjective dimension to knowledge. Tacit knowledge is personally and socially embedded; it is related to hunches, insights, intuitions, feelings, imagery and emotions. It is personal knowledge that is deeply rooted in an individual's experience and consciousness and is fashioned by his or her experiences, values and culture. It is the knowledge that helps individuals make sense of their world and as such is often deeply affected by their personal beliefs and values. It is knowledge that is felt.

Tacit knowledge has a crucial role in the organizational context and plays an important part in understanding knowledge management. Ikujiro Nonaka and Hirotaka Takeuchi are the writers who have done most to link the concept into managerial theory. They apply the notion of tacit knowledge to the organizational context in their book *The Knowledge-Creating Company* (1995), restating the classic distinction between tacit and explicit knowledge (explicit knowledge is objective and easy to transmit, while tacit knowledge, or *knowing how*, is more intangible and harder to explain to others). They argue that tacit knowledge is the source of expert judgements, and is as such of crucial importance to organizations.

Ikujiro Nonaka and Hirotaka Takeuchi also demonstrate that experience is the source of action. However, because it is subtler and more difficult to quantify and capture than explicit knowledge, it is very difficult to manipulate and manage. Tacit knowledge is the sum total of the actions, experiences, ideals, values and emotions of an individual. An individual learns through experience how to do things – ride bikes, make wise investments, make strategic decisions, teach students – but they may find it difficult to explain their skill and judgements to others.

Tacit knowledge is often context-specific and can only be expressed and communicated to others through metaphor and by analogy. It is, for example, impossible to reduce a complex skill performed by an accomplished musician or an inspirational teacher into a series of rules or simple instructions. Tacit knowledge is more slowly acquired than explicit knowledge and it requires extensive *know-how*, which is the term used by Nonaka and Takeuchi for the technical dimension of tacit knowledge.

It may also be impossible to separate tacit knowledge from the activity, and this makes it very difficult to manage. Indeed, in *Enabling Knowledge Creation* (2000), Nonaka and co-authors George Von Krogh and Kazuo Ichijo argue that some knowledge may not be manageable at all. Their thesis is that knowledge management implies a control of processes, and that there are some processes and experiences occurring in organizations that are fundamentally uncontrollable.

One type of tacit knowledge, sometimes called *procedural knowledge*, is often the driving force behind the learning of a skill. It is knowledge of how to do something – speak a foreign language, play a musical instrument, or master craft skills as an apprentice. This type of knowledge is manifested in the motor and cognitive skills required in the doing of something. An explicit system of instruction may have helped a skilled person to learn in the first place but, once the skill has been mastered, the individual's understanding of their skill usually defies articulation. Such skills are inseparable from the activities themselves, and cannot be reduced to the type of information that can be captured in a database.

While hard industrial metaphors are employed to discuss explicit knowledge, the vocabulary associated with tacit knowledge is softer, using words such as 'nurturing', 'harvesting', 'creating', 'valuing', 'sharing', 'disseminating' and 'networking'.

Tacit or personal knowledge:

- is about 'knowing how' (procedural knowledge) (see page 14);
- is socially constructed knowledge;
- has two strands – technical knowledge or *know-how* and cognitive knowledge;
- contains the folklore of the organization;
- is stored inside people's heads;
- can be the knowledge of the mastery of a skill;
- contains values, insights, hunches, prejudices, feelings, images, symbols and beliefs;
- can be chaotic;
- is difficult to codify and to store on databases and Intranets;
- is often difficult to communicate and share;
- is valuable and a rich source of experience and learning.

Important distinctions

It is sometimes said that the distinction between tacit and explicit knowledge is closely related to the difference between *knowing that* and *knowing how* (sometimes described as the difference between declarative and procedural knowledge). It is helpful to look at this distinction to make sense of the two concepts of knowledge. In his book *The Concept of Mind* (1949), the eminent English philosopher Gilbert Ryle made the classic epistemological distinction between k*nowing that* and *knowing how*. He distinguished between knowledge that is rule-based and knowledge that is built up through experience.

For Ryle, *knowing that* is knowledge that is formalized, readily transferable and consciously accessible. It is the process of understanding basic principles, and such knowledge can be discovered by explicitly reflecting upon rules, ideas and underlying concepts. Such explicit or declarative knowledge is relatively easy to articulate and to communicate. This type of knowledge contrasts with *knowing how*, which is knowledge built up from direct personal experience of the world, and allows people to work skilfully without deliberate or forced attention. This experiential form of knowledge allows us to operate, make judgements and do things without recourse to the underlying rules or principles that are involved in taking action. While *knowing that* only gives us the facts, *knowing how* enables us to build up the knowledge via experience and can be learnt by applying our knowledge in novel and creative ways. The distinction is between having a skill developed through experience, such as knowing how to drive a car (*knowing how*), and understanding facts about driving, such as understanding the Highway Code or being aware of the speed limit (*knowing that*).

Both Polanyi and Ryle demonstrate that tacit knowledge and *knowing how* are different dimensions from explicit knowledge and *knowing that*, and that one cannot be reduced to the other. Ryle argues that *knowing how* does not produce *knowing that*, while Polanyi's argument is that no amount of explicit knowledge can provide a person with the insights and experience inherent in tacit knowledge. To produce actionable knowledge, practice and experience are required. Information by itself is not sufficient. You cannot learn to drive a car by reading a manual or studying the Highway Code.

The nature of knowledge may have an important cultural base, too. Nonaka and Takeuchi (*see above*) believe that the distinction between tacit and explicit knowledge represents the cultural differences between Japanese and US attitudes and approaches to doing business. They argue that Japan places more value than the United States on corporate knowledge, and that the Japanese are more inclined to value tacit knowledge. The Japanese have a business culture of continuous improvement and innovation and this path of *kaizen* has led them to value highly intuitive, ambiguous and non-linear ideas. They are able to convert tacit to explicit knowledge, through their team and quality circle approach, capturing crucial insights into the business process.

By contrast, the US approach is more mechanistic, preferring rational, logical and quantifiable data and are less likely to innovate, providing that current solutions work. There is a culture of 'If it ain't broke, don't fix it'. Nonaka and Takeuchi see businesspeople in the United States as exponents of explicit knowledge. They argue that their reliance on explicit knowledge places the US economy at a long-term disadvantage, as innovation is the key to business success in the knowledge age.

If their theory is right, developing the intuitive side of an organization's knowledge is clearly an important element in its long-term success. It requires the same degree of thought that is given to the development of those vehicles that propel explicit knowledge – Intranets, corporate databases and data warehouses.

Managing tacit knowledge

The distinction between the two concepts of knowledge has practical implications for its management. Understanding the distinction helps an organization analyse the nature of the knowledge at its disposal. It enables it to understand the importance of tacit knowledge, but it also requires it to understand its limitations. Explicit and tacit knowledge each require different forms of management. While tacit knowledge lies at the heart of an organization, it is highly personal, and it is difficult to use effectively. It requires a particular management approach and a thorough understanding of the psychology involved.

Management needs to focus on understanding the dynamics and the psychology of personal knowledge. Tacit knowledge is difficult to control in a predictable way. For example, employees may see the knowledge they possess as their own intellectual capital. They may feel no obligation to share it with others in the organization. They may see it as personal and private.

There are many disincentives to knowledge-sharing in most corporate cultures. In many organizations, individuals perceive their greatest value to be what they know. For them, knowledge is power. Their unique information gives them status, and often guarantees that they are listened to and consulted. For some, it is their insurance that they remain in employment. If they share their knowledge they may erode their personal value within the organization, or they may be beaten to a promotion by the person with whom they shared that knowledge. The other person may use their ideas as their own. Once their knowledge is in the public domain, they may no longer be seen as valuable or important.

The problem is compounded in a climate of redundancy. After a downsizing exercise, the employees who remain will be very wary about being too public with what they know. They may see their personal knowledge as their only form of personal power in an uncertain and fragile future.

Managing knowledge is as much about good people management as about information and data processing. Processes need to be found to make tacit knowledge communicable and available to as wide an audience as possible. Harnessing tacit knowledge requires excellent management, interpersonal and communication skills as well as a good IT infrastructure. Realizing the potential of tacit knowledge involves an enormous culture shift and is a much bigger project than just investing in information technology. It is about trusting and valuing employees.

Simply listening to people talk about their personal knowledge is an important activity in an organization and is the reason why appraisals, performance reviews, feedback sessions, mentoring, exit interviews and other good HR practices are so important. Work teams and more informal networking and mentoring groups can also be a very useful means of sharing tacit knowledge. As organizations grow, it becomes increasingly unlikely that word of mouth will be an adequate means of conveying all the tacit knowledge that needs to be shared. There will be a need to find more formalized means of sharing. Action learning projects, as part of a learning organization initiative, are good, with an enquiry team investigating an issue and reporting its finding back to a wider group. This is particularly powerful if the enquiry team is a cross-level, cross-corporate group.

It is important for an organization to have methods for exploiting tacit knowledge. While conversations and meetings are the main means of doing this, the importance of tacit knowledge is too often insufficiently understood. This is particularly the case with the tacit knowledge held by those in the supply chain and by stakeholders. Their knowledge is often partial, individual and situational. It often relies on anecdotes and is usually not shared through formal channels. It presents particular challenges – how is it possible to manage something so ephemeral?

Whatever the difficulties, organizations should not give up on trying to share the tacit knowledge contained within them, but they should not attempt to treat it like explicit knowledge. They need to find ways of making tacit knowledge more explicit so that it can be more readily shared. They need to build the structures that will make people enjoy sharing their knowledge. This often involves positive rewards for knowledge sharing, giving a value to this practice.

Managing tacit knowledge causes all sorts of methodological and practical problems for any organization. Knowledge may be a thing, but it is also an activity and a process. Tacit knowledge is diverse, personal and subjective. It is not easily measurable and difficult to quantify. It does not lend itself to systematic data capture. Nevertheless, it is an invaluable source of an organization's intellectual capital. While most senior managers believe in the importance of interpersonal relations and people-to-people communications, it causes immense problems if they are required to believe that this should be a major source of organization knowledge. Many managers resist the prospect of augmenting explicit knowledge with softer and less tangible sources of information.

Trying to ground an organization in its informal structures is sometimes a very problematic undertaking. Equally problematic is the task of making tacit knowledge explicit so that it can be more easily shared.

Learning conversations

Tacit knowledge is based on insights and personal experiences. It can be uncertain and personal, and a sometimes chaotic form of knowledge. It is difficult to capture and use effectively and the knowledge conversion and sharing processes can be problematic. On an individual level, acquiring tacit knowledge is about how people organize their own world and acquire important informal competences. On an organizational level, tacit knowledge can contain much important information about what makes the organization tick. It is a rich source of information via which an organization can learn from its successes and failures.

However, there is a problem with managing the process of tacit knowledge creation. Many senior managers are either unaware of its significance or are uncomfortable with trying to use it. Even if managers realize its importance, many will feel that tacit knowledge is so ephemeral that they cannot see how to exploit it and use it successfully. After all, personal knowledge and experience are developed through social interactions, power plays, teamwork, friendships and corporate politics. It is very difficult to externalize these experiences and to draw meaningful conclusions. On the other hand, all this personal and ephemeral knowledge flows directly from the organization's culture. It is the human face of knowledge, and can provide the organization with an altogether different perspective from the one provided by its explicit knowledge.

An organization ignores this source of knowledge at its peril. The solution is not to dismiss tacit knowledge as too difficult to handle, but to find ways to make personal knowledge more generally accessible and easier to manage. One answer to this problem is to use a technique known as *storytelling* or *learning conversations*.

Learning conversations and storytelling – or *learning histories* and *organization dialogues*, as they are variously called – involve employees reliving in a structured way critical moments in the life of the organization. They can be said to be a *talking therapy* for organizations. The method is straightforward but powerful. It involves employees meeting together in a structured way and discussing what went right and what went wrong in particular situations. From this, they agree the lessons that emerge. The critical episodes are fully discussed, documented and evaluated. Learning conversations attempt to document events in such a way that the organization is enabled to learn from its own experiences. The organization communicates how it did things and the processes it used, but emphasizes the role played by individuals, and how they felt and acted in the process. Learning conversations can contain reports, surveys and notes of actions, but they also require personal and team evaluations and critical self-assessments. They can be used as a source of staff training and future decision making.

The critical-incident storytelling process requires employees to reflect on their experiences; the technique has much in common with action learning (*see* Chapter 5). Analysing a critical incident involves asking some or all of the following questions:

- Did the employees enjoy the activity?
- Were they surprised about the way they acted?
- Did it stretch them, excite or scare them?
- Have they developed new skills in the process?
- Was the outcome of the activity successful?
- Most importantly, what did they learn from the experience?

This process of tacit conversion involves bonding, sharing information and communicating best practices, success stories and failures. The storytelling is a social process, making people relive the critical incident as part of a process of evaluation. This approach also helps to overcome any fear of change. Many knowledge-management programmes fail because managers underestimate the fear of change and the unknown among their employees. There is a danger that organizations become awash with their own propaganda and fail to recognize their own weaknesses as well as their strengths. It is difficult to propel people into the unknown, and to ask them to take on a new approach and attitude to their work. This is where critical-incident storytelling comes into its own. Change arises out of learning. Corporate storytelling can be a vital means of ensuring that there is effective corporate learning. Most importantly, it grounds any ideas and procedures that arise from it firmly into the people and culture of the organization.

Clearly, the storytelling approach has much in common with action learning. The experience of successful teams provides the platform on which the organization can build its collective memory. It provides opportunities for sustained conversations about the important episodes in the organization's life. It is vital to find a way of capturing the experiences of teams and making them explicit; the actual method or techniques used are not so important. With a schedule of learning conversations, there are methodologies in place to ensure that institutional or corporate memory is kept up-to-date, and that genuine learning takes place.

To be effective, any storytelling activities need to be well structured, with a good problem-solving agenda, and culminating in a report and an action plan, to take the learning forward. Time must be set aside for reflection. Decisions must be made about dissemination following a learning conversation. Who should receive the reports and what should be their purpose? How should this valuable self-knowledge be used? Defining the audience for the conversation is important. Does the organization have a magazine, or a bulletin board on the organizational Intranet, where others can read the stories? Are they discussed at conferences and meetings?

Storytelling and learning conversations:

■ are effective means of corporate learning;
■ ensure that organizational memory is expanded;
■ build teamwork and communities of practice;
■ help to overcome fear of change;
■ help employees reflect on their experiences;
■ promote the sharing of experience and ideas;
■ provide a time for reflection;
■ utilize the critical-incident method;
■ require an action plan to move on the process of sharing.

The synergy between explicit and tacit knowledge

Nonaka and Takeuchi argue that organizations are interested in knowledge management because, as well as being smarter in their use of embedded knowledge, they need to engage in knowledge creation. After all, it is new knowledge that takes the organization forward. They need to recognize that knowledge creation is dynamic, involving a spiral process of interaction between tacit and explicit knowledge. Linking them, and building on their synergy, is essential. The process of linking tacit and explicit knowledge is known as the *knowledge conversion process*. The knowledge conversion process has four elements, as described by Nonaka and Takeuchi.

Tacit to tacit

The first element is the sharing of ideas, which is a *tacit to tacit* interaction. This is classically what happens in the dynamics of well-functioning teams or between colleagues who have ideas in common. People talk about what is important to them. They feed off the ideas of others, and the collective experience of sharing knowledge is a powerful means of creating new ideas. Essentially, this is a learning process, and social learning is a major means of facilitating tacit to tacit knowledge conversion.

Tacit to explicit

The second means of knowledge conversion, turning tacit knowledge into explicit knowledge, is a different process. In the *tacit to explicit* process, ideas are turned into practical reality. Metaphors and analogies have a prominent part to play in this process. In a team situation, metaphor helps team members externalize their tacit knowledge. It helps others to understand it in a way that makes it possible to use in a corporate setting.

In his book *Beyond World Class*, Clive Morton gives a graphic example of how the tacit to explicit conversion takes place. He describes Barnes Wallis and his team working on the dam-busting bombs that would destroy Germany's hydro-electric capability in the Second World War. They came up with the idea for the bouncing bomb by conceptualizing how children skim pebbles across the surface of the water.

Explicit to explicit

Once knowledge is explicit it is easier to make the *explicit to explicit* transfer that is Nonaka and Takeuchi's third means of transferring knowledge. This combining process allows ideas to be shared, and to be tested. The knowledge is in forms that can easily be transferred, via a range of means, including plans, charts, research and development and technical papers. It can be achieved globally through the communications media or by learning in formal settings using lectures, workshops, published papers, conferences, and seminars.

Explicit to tacit

The fourth and last means of knowledge conversion – the *explicit to tacit* conversion process – is more difficult. It is about the internalization of knowledge. It can help teams form mental images of the problems that need solving. This allows participants to bring their intuition and experience to bear on the issues. It is through the explicit to tacit conversion process that employees can act upon good ideas.

Internalization is very important in building understanding and developing a learning culture. Nonaka believes that the key to innovation is the social interaction that comes from socialization. Good socialization allows people to draw on their experiences (tacit) and to come up with new and novel solutions to problems that can be introduced for the benefit of the organization (explicit). The actual techniques of internalization are probably less significant than the bringing together of teams in both structured and semi-structured ways to allow them to honestly share and develop ideas and thinking. Many traditional and well-tried team-building approaches such as brainstorming lateral thinking and action learning can be effective in this knowledge conversion process. In the chapter on learning organizations, we discuss in more detail some of the means that can be employed to develop organizational learning.

Strategies for knowledge creation

In *Enabling Knowledge Creation*, Nonaka, Von Krogh and Ichijo argue that the fragility of knowledge creation means that it needs to be supported by a range of strategies. For each of the sequences in the knowledge-creating process, a range of enablers are employed. The knowledge process moving from sharing tacit knowledge to cross-levelling knowledge (essentially, developing a new idea or product). It is important to follow a framework that involves instilling a vision, and moves from managing conversations through to mobilizing activists, and creating the right context for knowledge creation to take place. Lastly, it is important to globalize local knowledge and ensure that it is shared widely throughout the organization.

The knowledge conversion process

▮ Tacit to tacit – the sharing of ideas that results from socialization
▮ Tacit to explicit – the emergence of new ideas from metaphor and analogy
▮ Explicit to explicit – combining knowledge to test ideas
▮ Explicit to tacit – developing new ideas and learning by doing

---

The implications for education

Releasing and utilizing tacit knowledge is a means of increasing the capacity of the organization, but it requires certain strategies. Without such strategies there is a danger of organizational amnesia; organizations forget what they have learnt, what they have done and why they have done it. E-mail, bulletin boards, chat-lines and software such as Lotus Notes and Microsoft Outlook open up the possibilities of disseminating tacit knowledge to a wider audience; non-IT solutions, including focus groups, learning conversations, scenario planning and good old-fashioned well-run team and staff meetings, are just as important.

Education is well placed to use learning conversations and storytelling in a coherent fashion as a means of harnessing tacit knowledge. The extensive use of teamwork and collaborative learning in education gives institutions a head start, particularly as the processes of validating, verifying, and examining programmes provides the basis for building up the basis of learning histories. This is particularly the case when institutions are using the techniques of self-assessment for reflecting on the strengths and weaknesses of their performance.

Educational learning conversations will contain not just reports and action plans but also the underlying assumptions and reactions to what has occurred. In building up a learning history it is important not just to capture the explicit knowledge, but also to encourage team members to share and make explicit their tacit knowledge, and apply it to new situations. Much of the education process is about the building up of tacit knowledge, especially in relation to the process of pedagogy. It is also crucially about building up the networks to help share, and importantly to make sense of that knowledge. If this is to be a success, time needs to be allocated for this type of reflection. Too often, meetings have to do with the business of education – assessment, student progress, evaluation and planning. Learning conversations are different. They require the team to have a more free-flowing conversation, unhindered by the normal tight agendas.

In these situations, a methodology such as Edward de Bono's 'six thinking hats' for creative thinking can provide a useful structure. This involves each member putting on a different 'thinking hat' for a period of the conversation. Typically, a conversation could start with members using 'red hat thinking' to give their emotional response to an issue, and follow this by 'black hat thinking', to look at what typically could go wrong. The next stage could be 'white hat thinking', to look objectively at the situation. While there is no right order for this process, the next stage could involve 'yellow hat thinking' for considering optimistic options, and 'blue hat thinking', to look at what information needs to be considered before the creative and lateral-thinking 'green hat' stage. These methodologies build upon the *emotional IQ* of their members – their members' ability to use their talents cooperatively to solve problems and to create new ideas. The aim is to help them to work without friction and self-interest for the common purpose of the group.

Knowledge communities

It is important to understand that knowledge is often built up and generated by informal, self-organizing networks of practitioners. In order to carry out a wide range of tasks, staff in educational institutions need to be able to call on loose networks of their co-workers. These ad hoc groups can have a wide range of talents, skills and competences, and the success of the group is often the reason for the success of a project. John Seely Brown of the Xerox Corporation and Paul Duguid talk in a commercial context about how sales representatives can build up small groups, or *communities*, united by common practice, to share their knowledge for their mutual benefit. They call these *communities of practice*, an idea also developed by Eric Lesser and Laurence Prusak, who define communities of practice as *knowledge in action*. These small informal groups of employees – what Von Krogh, Ichijo and Nonaka call *micro-communities of knowledge*, meet to share knowledge and work together to solve problems. We prefer to call them *knowledge* or *learning communities*.

Knowledge communities are not new. After all, groups of like-minded people have always met to share experience. However, they are often neglected in organizational cultures. In the traditional organizational setting they are seen as a distraction from the business in hand, or a means of time-wasting; the traditional common room conversation is one example. In fact, the opposite is the truth. Such informal networks and communities can often be of more benefit than formal committees and task groups.

Knowledge communities differ from work teams in that they are not formal or task-orientated. Instead, they are self-organized networks, and their organization makes sense to their members. They are often brought together by common interests, with a common need to share and communicate ideas and expertise, and to solve problems. They develop in the social space between formal hierarchies and project teams.

Communities exchange and interpret information, build expertise, and act as repositories of knowledge. They can create new knowledge and ideas that can keep the institution at the cutting edge. Theirs is a form of collective intelligence, which builds and develops tacit knowledge. Typically, knowledge communities develop around issues that matter and have an important role in knowledge management and creation. They are extremely good at solving problems, particularly those that are unexpected. Formal structures are often not good at the difficulties that arise out of the blue, while informal networks are highly adaptable because they do not have to follow the protocol of the educational hierarchy.

Knowledge communities in education are particularly important in nurturing and harvesting tacit knowledge and in building up a sense of common purpose, although they can be equally valuable in creating explicit knowledge. They can work as well with contracts, regulations and codified procedures as with rules of thumb, intuition, hunches and underlying assumptions. Etienne Wenger has argued that they have three defining characteristics. First, they have a sense of joint enterprise. This relates to more than simple goals; it reflects the members' understanding of their situation and gives exercises meaning. Second, members are bound together into a social entity, which Wenger calls 'relationships of mutual engagement'. Third, members bring a shared repertoire of communal resources to the party, including stories, past learning, tools, vocabulary and help for others. These are of direct benefit to others in the community, helping them to solve problems and improve their knowledge. As Wenger puts it:

> *Members of a community of practice are informally bound together. . . the value members find in their interactions is not merely instrumental. It also has to do with the personal satisfaction of knowing each other, of having colleagues who understand each other's perspectives, and belonging to an interesting group of people. (Wenger, 2000)*

Knowledge communities often span boundaries, but may also be found within a department or division of a school, college or university. They are likely to be cross-divisional or cross-functional, and may be intra- or extra-institutional. They are increasingly likely to be digital and, while they are primarily social, many communities of practice are now global. Such communities work outside the formal structures and overlap with them, but need to be supported by managers so that the learning generated by them can be effectively utilized. A nurturing leadership style is needed to make the best use of them in an educational setting, because they are potentially fragile.

The life cycle of a knowledge community depends on the importance its members place on the task at hand. Typically, they come together, develop, evolve, disperse, but often have no clear beginning or end. However, when a knowledge community disbands, much tacit knowledge is lost. It is very difficult to capture the lost knowledge because much of it is based around social relationships. It is, therefore, important that managers recognize the importance of such communities and take special measures to nurture their creativity.

Over time, communities can become more formalized, often losing some of their flair, especially if processes become too formalized. The important part of the creative process is not the minutes of meetings, but the ideas that come forward. However, to make network communities work, educational institutions need to make the resources available and to ensure that the work space encourages networking. Canteens, water fountains, drinks machines, common rooms and other shared spaces are vital in creating face-to-face encounters. Providing the facilities for electronic communication is equally important if the community is a virtual one.

Knowledge communities:

- are self-organized informal groups;
- have social meaning to members who value the relationships formed in the community;
- are learning communities;
- are built around common purposes and things that matter;
- involve the common pursuit of problems and solutions;
- operate across functions and divisions;
- can be supported by nurturing management and leadership styles;
- have a life cycle that depends on the value of the task to the group;
- are repositories of tacit knowledge;
- can make tacit knowledge explicit;
- can keep organizations at the leading edge of knowledge creation;
- can effectively use the emotional IQ of their members;
- can be supported by nurturing management and leadership styles;
- have a strong resonance in education.

Despite all the discussion about knowledge as the key to organizational success in the 21st century, very little is known about the best way of leveraging knowledge in practice, and about systematically creating it. Knowledge communities are probably one of the best practical means of developing and leveraging tacit knowledge, and many commentators see them as a way forward. Such communities can, of course, be virtual, with no defined geographical place. They are not a substitute for other elements of the organizational structure. They should not replace the more formal work teams or project groups. They are much looser networks, which colleagues form themselves. They are an important addition to the array of relationships in an organization, but specifically focused on leveraging knowledge creation. The glue of such communities is their communications mechanisms – it is through communication with colleagues that knowledge is shared. Knowledge communities are ideally placed to use communications techniques such as storytelling and learning histories to advantage:

The talk and the work, the communication are inseparable. The talk made the work intelligible, and the work made the talk intelligible. (Brown and Dinguid 1991)

The idea of knowledge community networks is one that has a strong resonance in education. Teachers and lecturers have a strong sense of their own worth and a strong sense of professionalism. They relate well to colleagues and use their peers as a sounding board for ideas. It may be that the knowledge community is the model for productive knowledge-sharing in education. The term 'community of scholars' is often used, but there is rarely any institutional encouragement or structure to help such communities flourish. Education needs to work hard to develop real communities of scholars.

2 Knowledge leadership

'Increasingly the act of management is managing knowledge.'

Chris Argyris

This chapter examines some of the key organizational and leadership issues that affect knowledge creation. Somewhat unusually, we look at leadership in the context of nurturing and sharing – the leader as mentor, nurturer and coach is not the set of metaphors that is commonly applied. In addition, we explore the structures that can incubate and foster knowledge. This perspective has only recently come to prominence in management literature. It challenges some of the main tenets of recent management theory, particularly the striving for flat, delayered structures associated with process re-engineering. In its place, we highlight a revival of interest in the role of middle managers, seeing them as potential leaders of knowledge communities. We also examine the role that chief knowledge officers (CKOs) can play as internal consultants to the process of knowledge creation, as well as the need for managers to recognize that they are now all knowledge managers.

Leadership issues in knowledge organizations

The main thesis of Peter Drucker's book, *Management Challenges for the 21st Century*, is that company executives must learn to manage knowledge workers. This is a new art with a new set of skills. Traditionally, managers have concentrated on producing an end product; today, they need an alternative focus. Their primary task is now to nurture and coach those who have the ideas, skills, technical ability and brilliance within their organization. For many managers, this change of tack will represent a culture shock. Many will not be able to cope, and will need to be trained by their organization in new management skills. Many will not recognize the change and will continue in the old ways.

All too often, organizations see employees as lacking in strategic importance, or as largely expendable. In the quest for greater efficiency, managers too often give their focus to systems and structures. Managing knowledge means managing people, and doing this in a way that allows them to give of their best. Drucker is of the opinion that almost all companies still manage their employees as though they are in control of the means of production. Today's reality is very different. It is the knowledge workers who exercise the control. They are the ones who really know about the product. They make the production processes work. Lose them, or demoralize them, and the organization is in serious trouble.

Recognizing this requires enormous changes for managers – in their role as well as in their mind set. No longer can they seek to control their organization in the old ways. They cannot manage knowledge as if it is a physical form of capital. Part of that change of mindset is an understanding that their organization's intellectual capital is based on the intelligence and skills of its employees. Leadership style has to change as well. Something subtler than command and control is needed, and this requires a high degree of personal mastery and self-awareness. Traditional forms of management have to be replaced by coaching and care. Managers need to develop the skills of encouraging and mentoring. Additionally, the power base of the organization shifts. The locus of control moves from corporate managers to the owners of organizational knowledge. A company may own patents, but the tacit knowledge of how things actually operate resides elsewhere. In such changed circumstances the leader's role is to create the conditions in which knowledge can flourish. Management becomes knowledge management.

There are many challenges in managing knowledge. Knowledge is not the same as a physical means of production. It involves intangibles that are difficult to quantify and capture. Knowledge may not even be manageable in the true sense of the term (certainly, Von Krogh, Ichijo and Nonaka have forcefully argued this point). But does that matter? After all, the goal for a successful knowledge-driven organization is little direct management, particularly the traditional type of management that seeks to exercise control. Knowledge workers are ideally self-managers.

An organization does not need traditional management, but it does need models of how to do things differently, and guides to how things have changed. There is a need for case studies about how to lead in a world where managers no longer have full and effective control, but where they encourage, foster and support a highly motivated workforce. This is not just an ideal for a new age; it is a reality in many professional and hi-tech enterprises. The free-nation agent ideas of autonomy, independence and writing one's own manifesto are an everyday occurrence in many organizations.

Over the past decade, Drucker has focused on the not-for-profit sector as the paradigm case of how to manage successfully in the knowledge age. In successful not-for-profit organizations, making money is not the primary motivation for the people. The job itself provides the interest and is motivating. Staff gain satisfaction from why, what and how they do things. The motivation comes from being challenged and valued, and the role of the leaders is to make the organization's mission the staff's mission. In a successful not-for-profit organization it is the staff who have *ownership*, in a real if not a legal sense.

Knowledge-age issues

▌ The organization is based around the idea that knowledge is a social construct.
▌ Knowledge, not physical assets, is the important means of production.
▌ Not-for-profit organizations may be the paradigm case for the knowledge age.
▌ Organizational leaders and managers need to understand the psychology of knowledge creation and transfer.
▌ Contemporary organizations must come to grips with the ambiguities of knowledge-age organizations.
▌ Leadership nurtures networks of knowledge communities.

Leadership of knowledge communities

There has been a considerable shift in thinking about organizational leadership in recent years. During the 1980s and '90s, the predominant managerial culture emphasized management at the expense of leadership. Despite the emphasis on leadership in the literature of total quality management, in reality, downsizing, rightsizing and process re-engineering predominated. The emphasis was on efficiency and cost-cutting and that required a command and control style of management.

Knowledge management takes a different perspective and requires leadership to predominate over management. More importantly, the style of leadership needs to encourage trust and sharing. The style, which is necessary to take collaboration forward, can be called *network leadership*. It recognizes that 21st-century organizations are professional and composed of intelligent and motivated people. Network leaders are the nurturers of knowledge communities. Once this is appreciated, style needs to follow function and the new breed of leaders will engage in enthusing and encouraging communities of experts and professionals.

Organizations that attempt to improve their knowledge processes often find themselves working within an interesting paradox. By necessity, they are rooted (some would say stuck) in the corporate world of management practice as it has existed for several decades. At the same time, they are exposed to the fast-moving but somewhat murky new waters of intangible assets and knowledge management. In the emerging body of thought it is possible to see both perspectives in play. On the one hand, there is the view that reflects the traditional management literature. This *technocratic view* believes in technical solutions. It has shades of Taylorism about it. The other, more radical perspective recognizes the ambiguities inherent in post-modern organizations, as managers strive to come to grips with the knowledge age. The traditional view fails to recognize the deep truths about knowledge cultures and the nature of tacit knowledge.

The technocratic view perpetuates a powerful myth that successful management is about delivering the right IT or other technical solutions. There is a risk that people who hold the technocratic view may reduce knowledge management to a *software solution* (believing that knowledge can be programmed to control the production hardware of the organization). In contrast, the *social construct* perspective on knowledge management sees knowledge as the result of interactions between stakeholders. This new thinking at its most extreme sees the organization as consisting of nothing but personal knowledge and knowledge flow. This requires an entirely different managerial mind set from the industrial era. Organizational success is no longer measured by the build-up of tangible assets, such as building and machinery. Organizations now require leaders who are sensitive to the psychology of knowledge creation and whose purpose is to nurture knowledge-creating communities.

Issues in network leadership

▌ Requires leadership not management.
▌ Recognizes that tacit knowledge is not strictly manageable.
▌ Nurtures knowledge workers.
▌ Recognizes that knowledge is a social construct.
▌ Acknowledges that knowledge workers are self-motivating.
▌ Requires leaders to encourage and enthuse knowledge workers.

Network leadership and tacit knowledge

Looking after tacit knowledge

An organization's tacit knowledge is deeply rooted in the feelings, emotions and personal values of its employees. It is the product of the culture and mores of the organization and is rarely formalized. It is difficult to capture and, as such, not easily accessible to a wider audience. Because it is personal, it is stored not in filing systems and databases, but in people's minds. This is why so much damage is caused when key individuals leave the organization. When people leave, a considerable amount of the organization's knowledge leaves with them. 'Brain drains' are becoming recognized as one of the major problems for modern organizations.

Many companies in recent years have used the delayering principles of process re-engineering, in the name of efficiency; ironically, rather than gaining greater efficiency, many have lost a substantial part of the knowledge that was essential to their operation. During the fashion for downsizing, many companies failed to understand the source of their competitive advantage. They thought they were increasing efficiency by losing substantial numbers of staff. In practice, they were losing skills, expertise and knowhow. Sometimes, their entire stock of intellectual capital was lost. They disposed of the people who knew the customers and suppliers best, who understood the processes and the way things were done.

Because tacit knowledge is intangible, many organizations failed to recognize its value. Downsizing and re-engineering exercises, including early retirements, voluntary and compulsory redundancies, have devastated organizational knowledge bases. Many organizations have, in effect, created their own knowledge vacuum.

There is now a better understanding of the importance of organizational knowledge, and of its fragile nature. The concept of tacit knowledge helps organizations to understand the social and existential dimensions of organizational knowledge, and its links to corporate culture, organizational politics, and the professional and private experience of employees. The management of tacit knowledge should be premised on the idea that much of an organization's most valuable knowledge is locked internally in the memory of its employees, and externally in the views and attitudes of its clients and stakeholders. Because tacit knowledge tends to be highly personal, it is often difficult to communicate quickly or effectively, particularly if it relates to emotional issues. Yet, intangible beliefs, judgements, values, prejudices, insights and intuitions are at the centre of the organizational culture.

Today, it is more widely recognized that the tacit knowledge of employees relates to a range of individual, social and historical circumstances. It is complex and is developed by employees over time. If that knowledge is to be used, it needs to be given a voice, an audience and a social setting in which it can grow. Recognizing these complex dynamics helps organizations to understand the value of particular employees, and the need for a strategy for each individual, to enable them to give of their best. Ignoring this is very risky. The knowledge of each staff member is very difficult to replicate, and it will leave the organization when they do.

Structure and hierarchy

The challenge facing organizations is how to bridge the gap between the way they used to organize themselves and the way they need to structure themselves in the knowledge age. The traditional organizational form involves a tightly constructed hierarchy that is managed and controlled centrally. Power is located at the apex of the organization and communication is largely top-down.

Knowledge organizations require a new structure, capable of accommodating learning organizations and knowledge communities. They need multi-directional communication channels and plenty of interactions in decision making. While traditional structures do a good job in developing organizational experts, they are poor at linking them and creating synergy with other experts in the field. The network leadership task is to create structures and climates that allow learning and innovation to flourish.

The term *climate* is very important in this process. Organization climate is not often referred to in management literature, but it plays a crucial role in the subtle world of nurturing tacit knowledge. Sometimes referred to as the *social ecology* of an organization, climate is about the work culture. It covers such crucial but often nebulous ideas as space, degrees of autonomy and trust. These are the qualities and values to which the organizational structures of the knowledge age have to respond. They have to ensure that knowledge is central to the agenda and that they enhance the creative process.

Building trust

Most organizations know that they will improve performance if their staff work together. But building collaboration is often difficult. Organizational life often encourages just the opposite. Instead of collaborating, many employees tend to be competitive and secretive. This combative individualism is due partly to habit, but it is also partly a response to the dominant organizational and societal norms. It starts at an early age. School examinations and the culture of grading and assessment, as well as many games and sports, encourage early individual competitiveness. While this develops many good qualities, it needs to be counterbalanced by collaborative activity. Otherwise, people learn that they get on better on their own. They feel that they have to differentiate themselves from others in order to succeed, and that possession of certain types of knowledge is one way of achieving this. In the work environment, certain types of performance appraisal and traditional merit pay systems promote a culture of individualism and competition.

Knowledge management requires a very different approach. It can be a daunting task to develop the type of culture that builds the desire for teamwork and where people see the advantages of sharing and collaborating. Staff cannot be cajoled or bullied into collaboration and teamwork. Building the right organizational climate, with policies to match, takes imagination and time. It is all about trust.

Personal trustworthiness

Trust is a crucial knowledge issue. However, building it is difficult and challenging. One of the best ways for organizational leaders to engender trust is to be trustworthy themselves, and to act with integrity. Trust grows out of acts of trustworthiness. Becoming recognized as being trustworthy is not an easy task and cannot be accomplished quickly. Managers sometimes find it difficult to build up staff trust, but Daft and Lengel (1998) identify a number of actions that can contribute:

▌ being honest;
▌ delegating;
▌ giving up control;
▌ encouraging people to participate;
▌ accepting ideas from others;
▌ relying on others;
▌ doing away with burdensome policies and procedures;
▌ focusing energy and enthusiasm on the success of the group;
▌ being prepared to share information;
▌ disclosing what you really feel about something;
▌ doing what you say you will do, and doing what you say;
▌ serving others;
▌ affirming, building and mentoring others.

Organizational trustworthiness

An organization's trust-building process has a number of linked stages. The first stage of building collaboration has its basis in the need to develop rapport. Groups, meetings and processes need to be established so that each employee can learn from the skills and expertise of others. At this stage, little technological or managerial control or interference is needed. It is a process of bottom-down sharing, with management encouraging and establishing the space for teamworking to develop.

The next stage is when members of groups become more focused and active. This is when the prevailing corporate culture can encourage group activities by rewarding innovative thoughts and action. At this time, management needs to encourage people to look outwards towards their colleagues, rather than inwards. Network leaders need to break down old habits and ensure that the trust required for collaboration can thrive.

Knowledge-sharing is a goal for any organization and the following stages of collaboration should help encourage employees to shift from hoarding to sharing knowledge. Techniques such as 'storytelling' and learning conversations (*see* page 18) have a vital role in this process. Technological infrastructures can also be useful for encouraging active collaboration.

To reach the next stage in the trust-building exercise, the corporate memory must be fully functioning. Staff need to have easy access to information, ideas and solutions, and need to know where old ideas can be unearthed and used again. Chat rooms, online communities and other inventive can be instrumental in supporting the sharing activities that build trust, and moving the culture to one of knowledge-sharing. As more and more people go online, informal communities spring up. Many organizations are now trying to harness the casual yet invaluable information that is gathered within these groups, who may have an interest in either the organization or in personal issues. Such communities allow important learning to take place; that learning works best where there is trust.

The final stage is rewarding the contribution of great teamwork. People are inclined to want some sort of scorecard that acknowledges their knowledge-sharing activity. Knowledge communities do not work like this. They depend upon the social relationships of the group, and notions about quantifying contribution should be avoided. The rewards should be personal – seeing that the contribution is appreciated or being able to take an idea from concept to fruition. Emphasis needs to be placed on employees' natural enthusiasm for their subject. Unlike some formal groups, which may feel isolated, collaborative groups are not cut off from the rest of the organization. And because they get the necessary tacit approval there is no 'us and them' mentality. In this way, both creativity and originality are preserved.

The structure of knowledge organizations

Many traditional structures are too rigid to allow for the most flexible use of knowledge. This can be a serious flaw. Structures have to allow for the acquisition, accumulation and exploitation of knowledge. This does not mean that hierarchy disappears. On the contrary, it is necessary to maintain essential bureaucratic operations, and to have structures that create and maintain policies and procedures.

However, hierarchies have their limitations. They need to be combined with looser and more task-orientated structures, with small teams and less formal (but none the less important) collaborative groups – Nonaka and Takeuchi call them the *knowledge crew*. They are also known as knowledge communities or communities of practice. Their importance is that they work against knowledge-hoarding, one of the most difficult barriers. They also prevent the organization degenerating into a series of fiefdoms and competing groups. Setting aside self-interest is a major step on the path to knowledge-sharing. Knowledge communities bring together ideas and provide an alternative outlet for organizational talents. They offer freedom and autonomy to their members and allow them to bring their intuition and insights to the table.

Knowledge communities are the *voluntary* side of the organization. While this may sound optional, it is not. In fact, knowledge communities are essential. They are voluntary because it is the employees who are the true owners of tacit knowledge; without their active participation, knowledge will not be shared or created.

Knowledge workers

In the knowledge economy it is important to allow talents to blossom. The free-nation workers of the knowledge age are the portable people who own the organization's key factor of production – the knowledge contained in their brains. New structures are needed in order to nurture these people. Ideas are the currency of the new economy, so organizations need to care for and nurture free-nation workers. Their knowledge has to be transferred from their head – from the tacit and the personal to the explicit – into new products and services. This is the purpose of the organizational structures of the knowledge age.

Properly nurturing knowledge workers requires a careful blend of autonomy and structure. Everyone needs a structure in which to work. However, structure too often equals *control*. In the knowledge age, structure has to equate to enabling, advising and assisting. And it has to be coupled with a freedom to grow, develop and be creative. Stifling bureaucratic structures reduce and even kill creativity. Free-nation workers have to be given the space to innovate and think. New structures have to provide clarity, and the social dimensions for knowledge creation and the building of knowledge and learning communities. Organizational hierarchies and knowledge communities offer parallel career ladders. As a result, structures are likely to be multi-layered and have to be designed to blend accountability with innovation.

Network organizations

Nonaka and Takeuchi describe the combination of hierarchies, with more informal teams and communities, as the *hypertext organization*. The hypertext (or *network*) organization can be said to exist when the non-hierarchical, self-organizing structure exists in parallel with the formal organizational hierarchy. It is called 'hypertext' by analogy, because hypertext consists of multiple layers of text, while conventional text consists of a single layer. Hypertext is complex, interconnected, and allows for multi-user operations. It is simply a metaphor for the complexity of the informal networks of social relationships that can exist in organizations.

The network organization is made up of multiple layers; some hold the organization's explicit and tacit knowledge, while others contain the values and goals of the organization. These layers supplement other structures, including business systems that exploit organizational knowledge, and project team layers that promote knowledge creation. The hypertext organization is a dynamic structure. It combines elements of traditional bureaucratic structures with task forces, and reaps the benefits of both. It enables staff to shift contexts. It allows them to move easily from projects to more traditional line functions and plays to individuals' strengths.

A network organization works best with a set of reward structures and management attitudes that are different from those in traditional organizations. It is more important to reward group activity than individual success, and to encourage autonomy rather than to exercise control. It involves a recognition that, in the process of knowledge creation, mistakes will be made and that these can be learning opportunities. It is also about tolerating and, indeed, encouraging the individual cultures that evolve in knowledge communities.

In a network organization, managers have to balance the needs of organizational policy with the culture of the voluntary communities, and find ways of blending them. They cannot dictate behaviour; instead, they need to find ways to stimulate and reward knowledge creation. They will have to work in a seemingly paradoxical manner and do so in a way that builds up trust.

Successful knowledge-management structures:

∎ are multi-layered network organizations;
∎ develop a climate of trust;
∎ recognize the needs of free-nation knowledge workers;
∎ promote sharing and collaboration;
∎ have organizational policies that promote working together;
∎ use middle managers as the knowledge conduit;
∎ have flexible teamwork structures that can generate the creative context;
∎ have a middle-up-down structure of communications (*see* page 40);
∎ develop knowledge communities and communities of practice;
∎ become network organizations;
∎ combine formal hierarchy with voluntary knowledge communities.

The role of middle managers

Once the pariahs of management theory, middle managers can now be seen as being central to the process of knowledge creation. Middle managers are at the very heart of an organization. They play the mediation role, interceding both between top and bottom, and between internal and external forces. More importantly, they are often the main knowledge creators. They act as team leaders and group coordinators. They are at the centre of knowledge management, as their role puts them in a position that intersects both the vertical and the horizontal information flow. They often lead knowledge communities and promote the sharing of knowledge.

This is a fundamental insight because, in delayering, and in the restructuring following so many re-engineering programmes, companies have often axed the post of the middle manager. In the flatter structures that were so fashionable in the 1980s and '90s, middle managers were actually perceived as a barrier to communications, and their roles were deleted.

Nonaka and Takeuchi, who have conducted fundamental research into the process of knowledge creation in Japanese companies, take a different view. They argue that the middle manager is essential to knowledge creation. They describe the ideal management structure for promoting knowledge management as neither top-down nor bottom-up, but *middle-up-down*. Rather than seeing these two styles as contrasting, they argue that the combination is the most helpful for knowledge creation. They champion the much-maligned middle manager as the lynchpin of the middle-up-down organization. (Indeed, it could be argued that the majority of organizational members are neither at the top nor the bottom of the organization, but operate somewhere between those ends of the spectrum.) The metaphors they use to describe the role of the middle manager are *knot* and *bridge*. In their link role, middle managers are seen as *knowledge engineers.* They create knowledge from the vertical and horizontal informational flows and are at the centre of the process of knowledge creation.

Of course, it is not just the role that is important. Equally crucial is the psychology and motivation of this group of managers. They will only be able to fulfill the role of knowledge engineer if they have a set of skills that enables them to be creative and allows them to recognize and reward creativity in others. Middle managers will need to be supported by an organization-wide strategy that enables the promotion of the learning and training that are so essential for knowledge creation, and particularly allows for the sharing of tacit knowledge.

Middle managers will play a crucial role in motivating staff to become the knowledge workers for the 21st century. They are ideally placed to fulfil the role of team leader and to build the trust among team members.

> Middle managers:
>
> ▌ are knowledge engineers;
> ▌ are in the centre of horizontal and vertical information flows;
> ▌ are the motivators of knowledge workers;
> ▌ are the knot and the bridge of knowledge creation;
> ▌ link the hierarchical and voluntary structures;
> ▌ build trust in teams;
> ▌ develop teams and knowledge communities.

Does education need knowledge champions?

'Leadership means creating the conditions that enable people to produce valid knowledge and to do so in a way that encourages personal responsibility.'
(Chris Argyris, 1998)

If an organization aspires to the creation of knowledge, it needs to have mechanisms through which knowledge leadership can be demonstrated and committed. New roles and titles, such as 'Chief Knowledge Officer' (CKO), are sometimes created. These titles, designed to demonstrate leadership, might sound pretentious. Does education need to have knowledge champions in place? Should they go down the route of appointing CKOs?

The important point to make is that knowledge has to be championed. In the relatively new role of CKO, it is the responsibility that is more important than the title. In a large organization, the CKO is the essential link in the programme of knowledge management, and gives it a voice on the senior management team. In many cases, CKOs are temporary or seconded appointments, often reporting directly to the Chief Executive Officer. Whether such a post is essential depends on a range of factors, including the size of the organization and how well it functions as a knowledge creator.

The CKO's role is to champion the knowledge-management programme. Knowledge initiatives inevitably require a champion and someone to draw together all the strands. CKOs need to encourage ideas and projects and motivate other employees to take part. Most importantly, they have a role in building up and supporting knowledge communities. Ultimately, the responsibility for knowledge management resides with line managers, but a new process requires a champion or internal consultant to lead and drive it. CKOs are change agents. They are there to help others to adapt, and to steer them through difficult periods of change. This can be particularly necessary with middle managers playing such a key role in knowledge creation. They are usually the most hard-pressed operationally and find it most difficult to find time for new initiatives. This group needs the help that a CKO can provide, in the form of a 'tool-kit' of ideas and solutions. When staff ask questions about how to develop this difficult subject called knowledge, someone needs to listen to them.

While a dedicated CKO is not essential, it is important to have someone within the institution to drive the process of creating a knowledgement-management programme and give leadership. Staff with busy professional lives need help to develop in a new field and may not have the time to drive a project themselves. Giving direction and encouraging change within the institution will be major tasks for the knowledge champion.

Knowledge champions:

▌ lead the knowledge programme;
▌ are internal consultants to the process;
▌ are change agents;
▌ develop a special expertise about knowledge issues;
▌ are the link to the senior management team;
▌ nurture knowledge creation.

Implications for education

One of the consequences of the downsizing trend of the 1990s was that staff became the forgotten army. The customer was king and there was a general feeling that employees could be downsized, outsourced or replaced by new technology. The knowledge-management thesis takes the opposite view. Rather than being a cost, staff are seen as the main asset of an organization, particularly if their creativity and intellect can be harnessed and if their motivation can be kept high. They are the organization's intellectual capital. Clearly, this is very much the case in education.

Rewarding knowledge creation

High-performance schools, colleges and universities need skilled, agile and innovative staff who are good at teamwork. Educational organizations need to recognize the value of their intellectual capital and the importance of the knowledge that their staff have. Appraisal and other feedback systems need to provide clarity about what is expected of staff, and to concentrate on staff contributions to knowledge creation. Appraisal systems need to be coupled to a proper system of rewards for those staff who enhance the organization's stock of knowledge and use it to creative ends.

Organizations need to show their appreciation of staff contributions to the institution's intellectual capital, but how can such contributions be measured? The value added by each professional is one measure, and this could include skills acquisition (ICT, classroom management, pastoral, marketing), as well as a willingness to undertake additional training and research output. Such intangibles as the quality of relationships and the ability to make personal networks and linkages also bring value to the establishment. Appraisals should avoid falling into the trap of ignoring tacit knowledge, and the psychology of its development. Staff must be allowed their right to meddle, create, initiate and feel empowered.

New roles for educational managers

In education, where change is endemic, collaborative working is a must and the development of personal networks and knowledge communities are essential. Staff need to be empowered and to receive ongoing training and development. The supporting infrastructure should provide both the right technologies and the right motivational and rewards package. Good knowledge management in education requires access to technology, to create, store and communicate, and to provide learning via the Internet. However, it is the development of personal networks that are the key to working in high-performance cultures. Networks provide the opportunities both for feeling empowered as well as for building and developing knowledge.

However, *contingent organizations* represent a major challenge to traditional management practices. Once staff recognize the power of their personal networks, they may tend to rely more on them than on hierarchical relationships. In today's increasingly global workplace, people are more often aligned to their professional identity than to their employer. They are mobile and increasingly transient. This presents managers with a serious challenge. It may make them feel insecure or even marginalized. It is not that they are not shown respect, but they may feel irrelevant in this world of personal and virtual networks.

In order to add value in a contingent organizational culture, managers need to change. They have to manage differently. This can mean putting knowledge at the forefront of their priorities. They need to embrace a style that encourages and can live with the ambiguity and paradoxes that networks bring about. This can sometimes be uncomfortable, especially for those managers who find it difficult to understand colleagues who see themselves as free-nation entities. However, technology can provide managers with new ways to manage. In the past, monitoring was a major reason why managers could not 'let go' and delegate more. With improvements in technology, feedback can be in real time, allowing managers to ease off the reins and to trust their staff more. This sort of style will produce more empowered staff and will allow a real flowering of genuine professionalism.

Championing knowledge

One new role for educational managers is that of *knowledge champion*. It is often useful to have someone driving a new initiative, which is why knowledge initiative officers have been appointed in business. Championing knowledge should not be a sideline, but constitute a core activity alongside curriculum and resource management in any educational establishment. If knowledge management is to have a sufficiently high profile, it needs its champion. Most educational establishments will not be able to dedicate a role to knowledge management, but giving a senior member of the team the responsibility, or creating a secondment, may be a way of taking the process forward.

An establishment's knowledge champion needs the skills of teambuilding, inspiration and network leadership. There is also an important ambassadorial role, because not all members of staff will see knowledge creation and knowledge sharing as their number one task. They will need to be brought on board.

The role will not focus on technology (the IT issues can continue to reside with the IT department), but on building a sustainable knowledge culture. It is the vision, strategy and the ability to facilitate human change that develop a knowledge-sharing culture. Good management is about people, but managers need the tools (particularly the technological tools) if they are to do the job well.

Caring for knowledge workers

A second new role for managers is that of *knowledge carer*. Work is becoming increasing difficult, challenging and stressful. Demands on workers are increasing, and will multiply, and there is a danger of burn-out in key knowledge workers. A combination of fast-changing work practices, coupled with increased accountability, is undoubtedly leading to more pressure and stress. While it is clearly important for managers to look after knowledge, they also need to look after the people who create and use it.

Taking the pressure off rather than adding to the load is a major role for the new-style managers. Finding new and simpler ways of doing things also helps. Managers also need to find ways of reducing stress, and giving teachers more time for their core activities is all part of the role of a knowledge carer. It is important to ensure that staff can properly manage their work–life balance. It is now so expensive to recruit and train staff that it is important to look after them, especially the high achievers. One aspect of their care is to keep them creative and engaged. They need not just job satisfaction but a reason to stay with the organization and to keep enjoying the experience of working there. They need to be able to do what they are best at. This provides a major challenge because it is an issue of resource management that is rarely considered. Knowledge care is likely to be a topic of major concern in the world of 21st-century education.

Leaders need to develop excellent frameworks within which to manage knowledge. Traditionally, education is not good at the management of procedures and processes. There is a certain disdain for structure among educators. They are often not good at some of the process mechanisms that are essential for good knowledge management. While creativity is vital, it needs to be balanced with good processes for management and sharing. The transfer of knowledge relies on excellent communication and the mechanisms need to be in place so that it can be shared. None of this can happen without management and structure. The 'contingent organization' is contingent upon the management of good processes, but also upon the motivation of employees to be creative and to sparkle with ideas and new possibilities. Each needs the other and relies on the opposite effects of the other. When the institutional culture is grounded in such a shared vision and values, a stronger performance usually occurs.

3 Models for making the best use of knowledge

'. . . knowledge accumulates slowly, over time, shaped and channelled into certain directions through the nudging of hundreds of daily managerial decisions.'

Dorothy Leonard, *Wellsprings of Knowledge (1995)*

This chapter explores some of the key issues involved in classifying, auditing and accounting for an organization's knowledge. These are important issues because they address the organization's need to *know what they know*. We will follow this by proposing our own model framework for the management of knowledge, and continue by considering the implications for education of applying the framework.

The important issues include the following:

▮ Classifying knowledge ('If only we knew all that we know.')
▮ A framework for knowledge ('Knowing what we know.')
▮ Auditing knowledge ('Assessing what we know.')
▮ Accounting for knowledge ('Measuring what we know.')
▮ Technology and knowledge management ('Applying what we know.')
▮ The implications for education ('Exploiting what we know.')

Classifying knowledge ('If only we knew all that we know')

There are considerable challenges involved in properly managing an organization's knowledge. After all, the success of any organization may depend on how well it uses its knowledge and creates new knowledge. Before we can manage existing knowledge and create new ideas we need to know all that we already know. For this to be possible, a framework and system for classifying knowledge is needed. The assumption is that classifying knowledge is relatively easy; in reality, knowing all that we know is a complex exercise.

Classifying knowledge involves asking some fundamental questions about the organization. Developing the knowledge taxonomy has to be part of the organizational strategy and purpose. It assists in transmitting the corporate memory; this is tricky, because means have to be found to transfer tacit knowledge into the collective memory. To be able to classify knowledge successfully, organizations have to understand the dynamics and complexities of their own processes of knowledge creation. Codifying organizational knowledge helps organizations to understand the dimensions of knowledge, and the range of its uses.

In libraries and bookshops, or on teachers' shelves, knowledge can be conveniently located via subject – history, geography, chemistry, engineering, and so on? Even the ground-breaking Internet classifies much of its knowledge in this traditional subject-based way. However, before going to the trouble of capturing and classifying knowledge, it is important to think about the potential uses of that knowledge.

There are multiple ways of classifying knowledge and many have little to do with content. Knowledge might be classified according to where it can be found, according to its value, or according to its anticipated obsolescence. It might be classified according to its use – strategy, client value, product development or organizational learning.

Some fundamental questions will help an organization to identify how best to classify its knowledge:

▌ Accessibility – how accessible is the knowledge?
▌ Creativity – who contributes most to the creation of the knowledge?
▌ Currency – does the knowledge have a sell-by date or a date of anticipated obsolescence?
▌ Decision making – is the knowledge in a format that aids decision making?
▌ Individual – does the knowledge reside with particular individuals within the organization?
▌ Learning – is the organization learning sufficiently from its knowledge?
▌ Local or global – how broadly does the knowledge apply?
▌ Marketability – how saleable is the knowledge?
▌ Planning – does the organization know how best to use its knowledge?
▌ Reliability – how reliable is the knowledge?

▌ Richness – how complex is the knowledge?
▌ Sharing – how easy is it to share with others?
▌ Stakeholding – who makes the most use of the knowledge?
▌ Validity – how valid is the knowledge?
▌ Value – how valuable is the knowledge?

This list is not definitive; the point is that knowledge should be seen as multi-dimensional, and something that adds value. Indeed, one of the best uses of knowledge is as a means of becoming aware of what we know, or of becoming conscious that we now know something that we were previously unaware of.

Within any organization there are four states of awareness (*see* Figure 3.1). An organization can plot where it is against each one of the quadrants and may occupy more than one quadrant, depending on the range of its activities. The matrix can be used as the starting point to identify the strategies required for moving to a more desirable quadrant.

The organization is aware of what it knows ▌ The knowledgeable organization	The organization is aware of what it doesn't know ▌ The knowledgeable organization
The organization doesn't know what it knows ▌ The ignorant organization	The organization is not aware of what it does not know ▌ The ignorant organization

Figure 3.1 *Classifying organizational knowledge – if only we knew all that we know*

A knowledge-management framework ('Knowing what we know')

A model knowledge-management framework provides a means of working systematically through the issues involved in knowledge management. It also provides the opportunity to sort know-how in an organized fashion. The framework is based on the premise that an ordered approach is useful. It can be combined with the self-assessment checklist in Chapter 9.

Each educational institution needs to build up its own framework in order to benchmark its progress. This will depend very much upon its particular sector of education and its individual strengths and weaknesses. Establishing this will help it to judge what will best drive its knowledge-management programme, and allow it to set standards and targets. All institutions already possess some level of knowledge management within their existing structure. It is important to recognize this and a formal knowledge-management initiative begins by raising the awareness of what has already been done. The framework also needs to be amended to recognize prior achievement.

Knowledge management is often treated in a simplistic manner, with general principles being applied to every aspect of the organization. Generic solutions can leave organizations with little or no real practical advice or encouragement on how best to change their own particular system. However, best-practice benchmarking is a useful middle ground for organizations that are starting programmes. Consultants Ernst & Young and Andersen Consulting have carried out considerable research in this area and are recognized as leaders in the field for their knowledge-management processes. Xerox is another company at the forefront, and Buckman Laboratories of Memphis, Tennessee, and Finland's Nokia are world leaders in continuous learning environments. Buckman Laboratories' Web site (www.knowledge-nurture.com), dedicated to knowledge nurturing, is available not just for its associates and customers, but also for the whole knowledge-management community. Its practices can be easily adapted for use by education.

While it is important to guard against generic solutions to complex problems, it is true to say that a number of common themes drive any organization. Principles such as the importance of leadership, strategy and teamwork are generic best-practice drivers. But others, such as maximizing intellectual capital or recognizing the contribution of knowledge to innovation, are specific to the knowledge processes.

Our model framework will help institutions to understand the factors that make up the knowledge process. However, managing and creation is a non-linear process; while the framework is useful, it should not be taken as a step-by-step process.

1. Understand the knowledge available to the institution.
This is a preliminary step and involves a review of the institution's current knowledge assets. In undertaking this exercise, the following questions provide a starting point:

■ What knowledge assets does our organization currently possess?
■ What is the most critical source of knowledge in the organization?
■ Where are our knowledge assets currently held and in what form?
■ What do those knowledge assets contain?
■ What use and relevance are our knowledge assets to the organization?
■ How accessible are knowledge assets to the people who most need them?

2.   The second stage in this section involves an analysis of the process of knowledge creation. The following questions need to be answered:

■ What, if any, new knowledge is being created?
■ Who is creating knowledge within the organization?
■ Where is this new knowledge being created?
■ How quickly is new knowledge being added?
■ When is knowledge being added to the knowledge base?
■ How accessible is this new knowledge to staff at different levels in the organization?

3.   This needs to be followed by an evaluation of the organization's knowledge base. This is a far more difficult exercise than it sounds. It goes right to the heart of the purpose of the organization, and requires some fundamental and maybe difficult thinking. It is necessary to answer the following questions in order to evaluate the current knowledge base:

■ What current knowledge assets have value?
■ Why does the organization need to develop new knowledge?
■ Does current knowledge add value to the organization and in what way?
■ What knowledge is required for the future?
■ Where are the gaps in the organization's knowledge?
■ Which assets are increasing in value?
■ What current knowledge assets are losing value?

4.   Introduce new systems to capture and use knowledge.
This stage follows on directly from the first one and involves rethinking processes and procedures. Technological solutions will be needed to satisfy the explicit knowledge requirements of the organization. The main questions that need answering at this stage are:

■ How do we go about acquiring new knowledge?
■ Will our culture support an emphasis on knowledge management and creation?
■ Can we reasonably borrow ideas or learn the lessons from others?

▌ Do we need to research new ways of doing things?
▌ What systems do we need to capture and manage knowledge effectively?
▌ How do these systems differ from those already in use?
▌ Will our current technology support new systems?
▌ Will we need to introduce new technology?
▌ How will we evaluate the robustness and validity of any new systems that we introduce?

5. Establish effective management of new knowledge systems.
While such management systems have to be robust, they require the users to be empowered, probably through teamwork, and to exercise a high degree of stewardship and ownership over the management process. To ensure that there are best knowledge-management processes in place, it is necessary to answer the following questions:

▌ What are our organization's formal and informal communication channels?
▌ What technology do we currently have and how is it managed?
▌ What in-house expertise can we draw on?
▌ What technologies and management systems do we need to introduce?
▌ What training and development will we need to give teams?
▌ What training and development will we need to give to all our staff managers?

6. Develop the motivation to share and use knowledge.
This involves the very difficult problem of trying to change culture and to break down the barriers to knowledge sharing, particularly the sharing of tacit knowledge. This may involve changing working practices, building up communities of practice and looking at both monetary and non-monetary incentives. Training and development can act as a powerful medium to build up the motivation and trust required for sharing knowledge. Some of the barriers can be removed by answering some of the following questions:

▌ What are the opportunities for using our knowledge assets better?
▌ What are the current obstacles to knowledge creation?
▌ What are the current obstacles, both cultural and organizational, to their use?
▌ How can we identify the factors that inhibit knowledge sharing?
▌ Do our work practices encourage knowledge sharing?
▌ How can we best promote knowledge sharing?

■ Do we have effective communities of practice in place?
■ How robust is our teamworking?
■ How can we motivate and empower staff to share knowledge?
■ What rewards can we introduce to promote better knowledge sharing?

7. Make new knowledge available and simple to use.

Staff will never make the leap to effective knowledge sharing unless knowledge assets are easy and simple to use. They have to be accessible and easy to communicate. To ensure availability, answers are needed to the following questions:

■ Is it easy for people to communicate within the organization?
■ Do the communication structures match the organization's needs?
■ Are there opportunities for informal *work talk*?
■ Do our structures allow for the development of knowledge communities?
■ Does the structure of the organization facilitate the sharing of knowledge?
■ Can we communicate easily using technology?

8. Maintain the currency of the organization's knowledge.

Obsolete knowledge clutters knowledge systems, making it difficult for people to navigate and to have ready access to information. Obsolete knowledge can be potentially dangerous, as out-of-date information can be wrong or misleading, and can lead to mistakes and errors. However, it is wrong to assume that new knowledge is superior. To ensure that know-ledge is relevant, systems of knowledge management need to be reviewed regularly, to ensure that they add value. The following questions need to be asked if the currency of knowledge is to be maintained:

■ How do we know if knowledge has passed its sell-by date?
■ Do we have a means of regularly reviewing the currency of our know-ledge?
■ Do we have criteria for deciding when knowledge becomes obsolete?
■ Who makes the decision about the currency of our knowledge?
■ Is obsolete knowledge regularly cleared from the system?

Auditing knowledge ('Assessing what we know')

Prior to commencing a knowledge-management initiative, it is helpful to perform a knowledge audit or self-assessment exercise. Through a series of interviews and corresponding analysis, the audit can identify key issues within the organization relating to the way knowledge is used and the factors that encourage and inhibit it. There are a number of common threads in nearly every instance when this exercise is undertaken. When knowledge is audited, the following questions need to be answered:

▌ What knowledge is required for our strategy?
▌ Are there gaps or gluts in our knowledge?
▌ Are there knowledge assets that are lying idle?
▌ How do we deal with obsolete information?
▌ Do staff know where to go for information, advice and expertise?
▌ Is there sufficient knowledge of existing information sources?
▌ Do we know about new and relevant information?
▌ Do we avoid reinventing the wheel?
▌ Do we share information sufficiently?
▌ Do we recognize the need to exploit tacit knowledge?
▌ Do we have the ability to implement what is already known?

A knowledge audit can measure the strengths and weaknesses of the institution. The audit can also suggest the best ways of processing knowledge. It will enable the institution to identify internal factors that may be inhibiting knowledge sharing. For the knowledge audit to have any merit it is necessary to add an evaluation of a wide variety of institutional practices and experiences throughout the organization, over the course of several months.

One way of conducting the audit is to use a self-assessment tool (*see* the checklist in Chapter 8). This measures elements such as corporate culture and leadership style, which are critical in analysing an organization's opportunities for knowledge management, while at the same time uncovering potential obstacles to progress. It also reveals idiosyncratic factors and influences in areas such as team structures and business processes, as well as their potential impact.

It is useful as part of the audit to target specific user groups, to find out their perceptions. Knowledge-management initiatives appear to fail at a rate of between 20 and 50 per cent; to prevent a project from becoming another such statistic, an organization needs to understand how ready its staff are to accept the knowledge audit. It is important to find out where and how knowledge is being created, and how it is being used. It is important for the institution to determine whether its knowledge is relevant to a specific business objective, and whether it is being created accurately. In particular, it is necessary to ask if people are actually using the knowledge once it is created, and whether the technology is available to support the process of knowledge creation. Soliciting responses from everyone in the institution may reveal views and ideas that are frequently overlooked but may be critical success factors. Ensuring that everyone is included makes it possible to plot the institution's strengths and weaknesses.

The audit could begin with a staff survey, focusing on the informal approaches to knowledge sharing that already exist, such as e-mail groups and knowledge communities. An audit can also measure levels of knowledge usage and communication, and determine the perceived value of current knowledge sources. These can be fostered and formalized by offering, for example, a bulletin board or chat room on the corporate Intranet, or appropriate physical spaces where staff can share and create knowledge.

The involvement of an entire institution eliminates the possibility that any one group's perspective will unduly influence the overall direction of the knowledge-management initiative. Broad participation also enhances the validity of the findings, and provides an opportunity to assess major opinion trends and see how the perceptions of users and owners of knowledge shape the institution's culture. In the end, it may not matter what management thinks. It is the institution's potential for knowledge creation that is important. The reality is revealed in the experiences and attitudes of the staff.

By conducting this research through, say, a Web-based survey, it is possible to obtain results quickly and identify groups within the organization that exhibit extreme positive or negative variances in each of the factors measured. Once the survey results are in, it is possible to arrange interviews and to gather qualitative information. The survey results will allow for the targeting of interviews, reducing interview time and costs. Discovering the 'whys' behind the 'whats' revealed by the survey can provide a range of critical insights into the positive and negative influences on knowledge sharing.

The audit needs to include an analysis of tacit knowledge sources and may uncover the importance of informal teamworking and community development. It may also uncover obstacles to knowledge-management initiatives, such as cultural differences across departments and teams. There may be discrepancies between management policies and management action. By identifying these strengths and weaknesses the audit can be used to modify systems and processes.

Accounting for knowledge ('Measuring what we know')

It is worth discussing the main principles of accounting for knowledge, in order to understand that a value can be placed on the contribution of knowledge to an institution.

Many knowledge-management commentators have pointed out the limitations of traditional accounting in this field. Traditional accounting values the tangible assets of an organization, with the emphasis on physical rather than knowledge assets. Traditional accounting was developed when physical resources were the basis of wealth, and the financial account truly reflected a company's worth. Today, companies are frequently valued at many times their book value. The figures are calculated according to the organization's intangible wealth, based on client relationships, the competence of staff and the value of ideas and creativity. In the knowledge economy, the balance of wealth has shifted from exploitation of physical resources to development of the 21st-century assets of knowledge and creativity.

The basic building block for an organization's hidden wealth is the concept of *intellectual capital*. The main component is the brainpower of the people who work in the organization. The concept reflects the value of employee knowledge and expertise, the confidence of the customer in the products and services of the organization, and the efficiency of the organization's procedures.

In recent years, the drawing up of statements of intellectual capital has become an important part of knowledge management. The idea is to shed light on the benefits of managing knowledge, and to show managers the measurable impact of their actions. However, there is a considerable problem with drawing up such statements. If the Nonaka thesis about the centrality of tacit knowledge is accepted, then it is almost impossible to measure the contribution of knowledge, as much of it is highly subjective and intangible, and largely outside of the control of management. It is impossible to measure it. But intangible assets should not be ignored; these tacit assets can be the major contributors to the value of an organization.

Even if the knowledge is explicit only, it is still difficult to put a value on it. Knowledge is not all of a type and the value of particular pieces of knowledge is not always obvious. Before any form of balance sheet can be drawn up it is necessary to have a clear definition of knowledge, and a good idea of its contribution to the strategy and future of the organization.

The intellectual capital of an organization takes a number of forms:

■ Human capital: the contribution of people to the organization, expressed in terms of skills, competency and contribution to creativity and new ideas. The contribution of the staff is the key to success, so this is a defining idea within knowledge. In traditional accounting, people are seen not as an asset but as an expense. Knowledge accounting turns this on its head. Similarly, training and development, in terms of knowledge management, make one of the most important contributions to developing staff competence.

■ Physical knowledge capital: the physical knowledge assets of the organization, comprising the sources of explicit knowledge (information in databases, as well as patents, trademarks, and so on). In universities, research is one such important source.

■ Client capital: the loyalty built up in customers and clients and the ability of the organization to create consumer satisfaction. In the case of education, this includes the satisfaction of students, parents and other stakeholders in society.

In a commercial setting, the value of an organization's intellectual capital, or *knowledge capital*, as it is sometimes called, is said to be the difference between the value of the organization, based on its physical, human and capital assets, and its market value. The market value will value the potentiality of the organization, and the market's assessment of its ability to have a competitive advantage in an increasingly unstable trading environment.

In education it is difficult, if not impossible, to make this computation. Often, there is no balance sheet and no market valuation, except in private or corporatized institutions. However, while it may be impossible to completely replicate the relative precision that can be achieved in a commercial setting, it is still worth attempting to measure the value of intellectual capital. The best way is probably to look at the contribution of education to the wider society. Estimating the value of the system's graduates to the economy can be one way of doing this.

The key concept in estimating the value of education is that of *competency*. Competence – the output of the system – can be defined as the ability of a graduate to act in a particular situation and their ability to learn and be creative as a result of their learning experiences. Competent people are able to handle change and add value in the economic and social situations in which they are employed. They are the output of the education system and the key knowledge input for employing organizations. The sum total of competent graduates is the contribution of the education system to the intellectual capital of a society. The starting salaries of graduates could be used as a proxy for competency, if a financial measure is required. Using such measures, each institution should be able to compute its contribution to the creation of society's intellectual capital.

Benchmarking can provide a relative assessment of institutional strength in terms of the exploitation of intellectual capital. Institutions can attempt to estimate their exploitation of intellectual capital compared with that of competitor or exemplar organizations. By comparing the relative performance of institutions, it is possible to demonstrate their relative fitness, especially if the exercise is carried out on a regular basis. Such an approach could apply to both tacit and explicit knowledge, although it is difficult to value their *relative* contribution.

Accounting for knowledge

▋ Traditional accounting values physical not knowledge assets.
▋ Traditional accounting views employees as costs not assets.
▋ Knowledge accounting is based on the concept of intellectual capital.
▋ Intellectual capital can be measured as the difference between market value and the value of physical assets.
▋ In education it is necessary to find proxy measures for the contribution to society's stock of knowledge capital.
▋ The competency of graduates is one way of measuring education's contribution to society's intellectual capital.
▋ Benchmarking can be used to compare the organization's relative contribution to the exploitation of its intellectual capital.

Technology and knowledge management ('Applying what we know')

Thomas H. Davenport has written that effective knowledge management requires a hybrid solution of people and technology (1998). One school of thought sees computers taking over the role of knowledge managers but, while it is true that no organization can manage its knowledge without technology, it is only a part of the equation.

Technology can provide the vehicles, such as corporate Intranets, for the successful management of explicit knowledge. ICT makes information easier to store, access and manipulate. It gives strength to the notion that all corporate knowledge should be easy to find and easy to retrieve, and that knowledge management is simply the application of technology.

Nothing could be further from the truth. Knowledge maps, data ware-houses, expert systems and other innovative technologies can improve information flow, and provide the potential for making much better use of the valuable resource of knowledge. But before technology can provide the solution, the organization has to decide who needs to know what and to classify the data accordingly.

Technology is good at some things, but less good at others. In some situations, technology enhances people domain processes. Computers are good at storing, capturing, structuring and distributing large amounts of information. They can produce standardized reports on such thing as student numbers, examination pass rates, graduate destinations, and are useful for providing data to government agencies. They also play an increasingly significant role as the main medium of institutional communi-cations (although there is much evidence that the overuse, or inappropriate use, of e-mail may create its own problems). However, these important gains sometimes mislead senior managers, who overlook the importance to institutional success of interpersonal relationships.

Technology can also aid the collaborative processes, and properly thought out technology solutions should be central to the creation and sharing of knowledge. The sharing of explicit knowledge is an increasingly important use of technology. Tacit knowledge can also be shared, via virtual network-ing and in virtual learning environments. The development of virtual teams or communities, which may be global, can be a major organizational benefit. Many organizations are developing in-house collaboration systems, based on Microsoft Outlook or Exchange, and on the sophisticated use of e-mail. Useful documents may be stored on internal Web sites, where they are easily accessed; the 'Public folder' facility on Microsoft Outlook is one way of facilitating this. Such methods can quickly build up a repository of know-ledge for sharing throughout the organization.

Some of the benefits of technological applications are as follows:

Intranets:

- allow the publication of information electronically;
- interact with the user, who is able to source knowledge;
- change work methods;
- facilitate transactions via automated work processes;
- allow collaboration and knowledge sharing internally and externally;
- build virtual teams and networks;
- allow for 'any place any time' education and training in the workplace.

The Internet:

I gives ready access to the accumulated knowledge on the World Wide Web;
I facilitates the establishment of global communities;
I is an excellent means of knowledge sharing;
I allows for fast transmission of ideas;
I gives access to e-commerce;
I gives access to e-learning;
I encourages independent learning at work and at home.

Data warehouses:

I integrate data across large organizations (such as an education authority or school board);
I create historical patterns;
I provide a combination of detailed and summarized knowledge;
I encourage codification of knowledge;
I encourage the asking of questions.

Remember, however, that data warehouses can easily become full.

Virtual learning environments:

I allow the creation of high-quality material by teachers;
I allow teachers to share high-quality resources;
I allow links to existing databases, particularly student records;
I allow online testing and assessments;
I enable the creation of specific coursework;
I enable the importing of high-quality commercial materials.

The implications for education ('Exploiting what we know')

The implications for education of the model framework depend upon the perspective being taken. It will need to be modified for various groups of people, for example, teachers, principals or local or national policy-makers. The perspective may also differ in relation to the nature of the educational organization. For example, the view from a small rural primary school may be very different from that in a leading research academy in a major university. As such, it is difficult to make any accurate generalizations about the framework. Nevertheless, there are some key points:

1. The process of classifying the knowledge of an educational organization, for example, in the 2 x 2 matrix (*see* Figure 3.1), may lead to formal recognition of a key opportunity or problem. The knowledge problem may be one that relates, for example, to student discipline. New ways of moving forward to support young people may only be found if there is a greater knowledge of the problems and its causes.
2. Using the knowledge-management framework and supporting questions, in either a systematic or informal manner, will provide opportunities to rethink processes. For example, are there enough opportunities for knowledge sharing and creation, in either formal or informal settings? Does the timetable or schedule of classes hinder or aid this process?
3. Auditing what an educational organization knows may seem a daunting task, but it can also be suprisingly liberating. It gives hard-pressed professionals the confidence to say what they know about their students and their communities. The knowledge can add real value to the learning experience and be the starting point for the development of a knowledge-rich community.
4. Knowledge has enormous financial as well as practical value to any organization. The problem lies in trying to realize this in public-sector organizations that do not have a market capitalization. There is no easy answer, but as recognition of the importance of intellectual capital accounting grows in the private sector, the more likely it is that the idea will be transferred to educational institutions.

Intellectual capital accounting provides important opportunities for education, because it is education's *products* – people with skills and competences – that are the building block of wealth. In the UK, New Labour were swept to victory in 1997, with Tony Blair pledging his commitment to 'Education, Education, Education'. The knowledge age makes education central to the well-being of companies, society and the economy. While this places an enormous burden on schools, colleges and universities, it also gives them the justification for investment in their infrastructure and staff. While some traditionalists may dislike the idea that knowledge has a direct financial value, its economic benefit can be used as a powerful argument in favour of increased resources in the education sector. Indeed, the argument has already been used to back the build-up of ICT infrastructures in education. And a recognition of the importance of technology in the knowledge age has led to important investment in education in developed nations.

The implications for education of our knowledge framework

▌ Learning can be any place, any time.

▌ There is remote access to tutors – online tutoring.

▌ Individualized learning becomes viable.

▌ Partnerships are encouraged – Cisco Systems Regional Networking Academies are excellent examples.

▌ Learning can be a global provision.

▌ It leads to the development of new programmes.

▌ New approaches to rigour and quality are possible.

However, technology does not replace good human relationships.

4 Adapting missions and strategies to thrive in the knowledge age

'Sharing and using knowledge are often unnatural acts.'

Thomas H. Davenport

No commercial organization today would be without its corporate strategy, its business development plan and its marketing, personnel and financial strategies. In recent years, organizations have come to realize the benefit of having quality and information-technology strategies, but few have yet to develop comprehensive strategies for knowledge management. And of the few that do have such a strategy, almost none are in the education sector.

On one level, developing knowledge-management strategy is like any other strategic activity, but there is another level at which it is different and special. Because knowledge is changing so quickly it is important to ensure that alternative scenarios are fully explored before a knowledge strategy is accepted and implemented.

This chapter argues that organizations should undertake a scenario-planning exercise as a prelude to devising their strategy. Strong links exist between scenario planning, organizational learning and the process of creating new organizational knowledge. The text follows with an explanation of the likely knowledge-management drivers, and ways that the strategy can be developed to take knowledge management forward.

63

Scenario planning

Scenario planning as an organizational development tool

Organizations have many developmental and learning needs. One important strand of learning that organizations need to develop is the ability to ensure their own success and survival. As world-renowned quality guru W. Edwards Deming said of the life-cycle of organizations, 'Survival is not compulsory'.

Scenario planning is a powerful tool for organizational learning and development, designed to ensure long-term survival and success. It has a relevance to education as it moves from the era of old certainties and into the world of continuous change.

Scenario planning is essentially a 'soft' tool. It combines lateral thinking with action learning in an attempt to model the possible futures for the organization. It requires a critical faculty and an ability to think creatively. Its purpose is to help the organization to adapt to change. It is a foresighting technique that harnesses the capacity of staff to imagine, and to learn from what they conjecture.

Scenario planning seeks to forecast how the world might look in 10, 20, 50 or even 100 years from the present, and to imagine the sort of future in which the organization may have to operate. From this, the organization can plan how it will respond and, most importantly, how it must adapt. Scenario planning is essentially an exercise in contingency thinking, but as a technique it makes its maximum impact when it answers genuine concerns and tackles real problems.

The technique was developed during the Cold War by governments preparing for nuclear war. The Royal Dutch Shell Company pioneered the technique in a corporate setting in the late 1960s, and used it to prepare for and respond to the oil crisis of the early 1970s. The company successfully predicted OPEC-controlled oil production and spiralling world fuel prices. In the 1980s, one of the scenarios written for the company predicted the opposite. It foresaw the dramatic decrease in oil prices caused by the discovery of new oil reserves in non-OPEC countries; it also predicted that energy conversation measures would be taken by consumers in response to the high oil prices of the 1970s, and that there would be a growing commitment to green issues. These predictive scenarios helped Shell to reposition itself. While other big oil companies invested heavily in oil and lost billions of dollars, Shell rose from fourteenth in the oil league table to second.

Today, many organizations have followed Shell's example and use scenario planning in order to understand the effects of the external environment on their business. They use it particularly when they are faced with the kind of monumental change that is brought about by economic, political or technological demands. This kind of change requires a massive response.

Creating scenarios

Scenario planning starts from the premise that it is impossible to know with any accuracy what the future holds. In order to find a robust strategy to meet an uncertain future, as many as four alternative strategies or scenarios are created. They can be mutually exclusive, but do not have to be. Each scenario models a plausible outlook for the organization, which could be its future. Each is a specially constructed *story* about organizational destiny.

The alternative stories are assembled from a wide range of stakeholders, including employees, customers and members of the supply chain. The more diverse the stakeholders the better, as this gives a greater range of thinking. Diverse people with common interests make the best participants. While there is more than one way of creating scenarios, experience shows that it is useful for participants to see a completely worked-up scenario beforehand, so that they can enter fully into the spirit of the exercise.

Participants are asked to formulate alternative explanations about the future of the organization – ideas about what might happen years ahead. The stories are not designed to predict the future, but to provide *insights* into what the future might hold. Participants are asked a series of questions about what might happen in the short, medium and the long term, to help them to focus on future events. They give their thoughts on optimistic and pessimistic scenarios, and are asked for their opinion on the factors that will lead to success or failure. A professional facilitator is often employed to keep participants enthusiastic and future-focused. Every 'What if?' is then gathered and built into a series of possible scenarios.

Taking part in the scenario-planning process can be a major aspect of organizational learning, helping employees to confront the opportunities and challenges facing their organization. The stories help the participants to think in a future mode and the exercise allows the organization to engage in a strategic conversation. It is a particular and special learning process; after all, the participants are the ones who will have to live in the future that they have in part created. The process also helps them to be collaborative and creative. They can change their minds freely if the future turns out to be different from the one that they imagined, because the scenario-planning exercise has already metaphorically taken them down a number of roads.

The building stage is key to the success of the whole technique. Scenarios are built by aggregating at a high level the forces that shape the organization's future. The way that senior managers develop the scenarios and evolve the future financial, human resource, and technological plans to meet them, is the important part of the exercise.

Stages in scenario planning

Scenario planning in organizations often has the following stages:

1. The process starts by engaging in a dialogue with significant and representative stakeholders, including employees. At this stage, open-ended questions are asked to encourage people to give frank answers. This provides the opportunity to develop ideas.
2. The second stage is the development of the agenda by an analysis of the questionnaires. The issues raised are then used as a basis for further investigation.
3. In the third stage, the focus is on the understanding of the underlying issues and cross-referencing the links between issues.
4. The next stage is to hold issues workshops, to explore the key issues that have been identified. Gaps for further research are explored.
5. After this stage, scenarios workshops are set up to establish the small number of possible scenarios that may represent the shape of the future in 10 to 20 years' time.
6. Lastly, the robustness of the strategy options is tested against the scenarios.

Scenario planning can work for any organization, provided that it has the time, resources and commitment of the management team. It is a very different process from traditional corporate or strategic planning, which is often merely an extension of a single vision. By contrast, scenario planning starts from the world that the organization is likely to inhabit. In fact, the term 'planning', which is usually used when there is a need to accomplish something, is rather inappropriate in the scenario-building process. The development of scenarios is more of an action learning technique. The activity stimulates and encourages organizational learning and opens up new opportunities.

Successful scenario planning

Scenarios are not predictions. Instead, they are visions of the direction that the future might take. There is no need to choose between scenarios. An organization may want to change or modify its policies to deal with more than one possible future.

Well-designed scenarios usually have the following features that make them successful:

- They are collaborative and involve a wide range of participants in the organization; the collective ownership of the scenarios helps to bind people together.
- A professional facilitator can help to keep the groups future-focused.
- Their timescale is long enough to make it possible to plan ahead for the future. Usually, the planning looks at least 10 years ahead, much longer than the traditional strategic plan.
- They are credible and the organization can respond to them and cope with them.
- They take account of changes in the external environment – both global and local – that will have an impact on the organization. They take account of increased globalization, converging technologies, the impact of IT, greater workplace flexibility, and the demand for greater learning and cheaper and more accessible information sources.
- They are neither too long nor too complex. They have a dramatic quality and concentrate on a few powerful stories about the organization's future. They bring the future possibilities to life in a memorable fashion, which helps the learning process.
- They number at least two, although as many as four scenarios may be developed.
- It is often said that the acid test of good scenarios is that they change vision, policy and behaviour. There is little point if the organization persists with the same view of the future that it had before.

The best outcome of scenario planning is a concise and visionary document that condenses the wide range of views that have been sought. The document dramatically illustrates the alternatives the organization has to face and respond to.

One of the founders of the technique, Herman Kahn, referred to the 'blind spot' of governments, who could not see that nuclear war could ever happen. It was for them that scenario planning was developed. While there is no best way to apply the lessons of the exercise, it should help the organization deal with its own 'blind spots', and free it from the shackles of its past.

The approach is about 'thinking the unthinkable'. It is a useful technique for keeping organizational learning alive and for preventing vision, as Kahn said, from becoming stale.

Scenario planning

■ Scenarios are imagined models of the future.
■ Scenario planning is based on 'thinking the unthinkable'; it is based on *stories* about what might happen.
■ Scenario planning helps an organization to focus on future events.
■ Scenario planning is linked strongly to organizational learning and the development of creativity.
■ Two to four scenarios are usually created.
■ The scenarios may or may not be mutually exclusive.
■ The scenario may throw future action into sharp focus.
■ There is no best way to apply the lessons of the exercise.
■ Scenario planning leads to the development of future possible policy.
■ Scenarios are a powerful means of adding to organizational knowledge.

Developing the strategic framework

After engaging in scenario planning, organizations need to put a framework in place, to assist them in moving towards the development of a knowledge-management strategy. The starting point is to classify and audit existing knowledge (*see* Chapter 3). The next stage, the scenario-planning exercise, provides the organization with a set of alternatives and helps it to learn from its current situation. The strategy-planning process should then include the following stages:

1. Where are we now?

■ Do we know what our needs are?
■ Do we currently have objectives to achieve in knowledge management?
■ Is knowledge creation and management part of our organizational mission?
■ Have we mapped our existing knowledge assets?
■ Do we have an inventory of knowledge sources?

▊ Have we tried to classify our knowledge?
▊ Have we carried out a systematic audit of our knowledge sources?
▊ Do we distinguish between explicit and tacit knowledge sources?
▊ Do we have processes for attempting to make tacit knowledge explicit?

2. How good are we at utilizing our current knowledge stock?
These questions are designed to help analyse the current way in which the current stock of knowledge is being utilized. A distinction needs to be made between *knowledge stocks* and *knowledge flows*. 'Stocks' refer to knowledge management, while 'flows' refer to knowledge creation.

▊ Do we have effective knowledge-management systems?
▊ Is our organizational structure knowledge user-friendly?
▊ Do we have a robust learning culture so that we learn from our knowledge?
▊ Is the creation of a corporate university a way forward?
▊ Do we have knowledge champions in our organization?
▊ Do we make an attempt consciously to leverage our knowledge?
▊ Do we make full use of tacit knowledge sources?

3. How can we improve our capacity for knowledge creation?
These questions, about the organization's ability to leverage knowledge flows, are intended to provoke thought and discomfort, and to provide challenges to the organization.

▊ Do we know what triggers our current knowledge-creation processes?
▊ Do we encourage our staff to be creative and innovative?
▊ How can we encourage greater organizational learning?
▊ How can we encourage greater individual learning?
▊ Can we cope if our people generate new and interesting ideas?
▊ Can we find ways to develop and support knowledge communities?
▊ Do we support our managers in the process of knowledge creation?
▊ Are there solutions that can assist in improving our knowledge-creation processes?

4. What are our future knowledge requirements, and how will they link to the scenarios for our future?
Following a scenario-planning exercise, it is important for the implications for knowledge management to be made transparent, and for the knowledge issues within each scenario to be properly understood. Answering the following questions will help this process:

▌ How crucial is the generation of new knowledge to realizing each of our future scenarios?

▌ Do we understand the knowledge-management issues arising from each scenario?

▌ What are our likely knowledge requirements for the future?

5. What are our priorities for the future?

The priorities for the future need to reflect the answers given to the questions in the above sections.

▌ As a result of the scenario and strategic review process, have we developed a set of priorities for the future of knowledge management?

▌ Can we translate these priorities into a set of milestones?

▌ Are these priorities in a format that can be easily translated into action?

▌ Have the priorities been communicated to staff?

▌ Are resources available to support the delivery of priorities?

6. How should we monitor the process of knowledge improvement?

Monitoring progress is notoriously difficult but it is crucial to the implementation of the strategy. The following questions will help keep the process on task:

▌ Have the improvements been a success?

▌ Do staff own the knowledge-management strategy?

▌ Have the improvements led to greater organizational learning?

▌ Has there been a noticeable increase in creativity?

▌ Has there been a measurable increase in knowledge creation?

▌ Do we have an increase in the number of knowledge communities and networks?

▌ Has there been an increase in the number of new products, services or innovations?

7. How will we undertake more fundamental reviews of our knowledge strategy?

While monitoring progress is important, it is equally important to develop a process of fundamental review. While monitoring should be a regular process, the reviews should take place at longer intervals. Fundamental questions should be asked about success or failure. If the strategy is not being achieved, this is the process for re-examining the strategy and putting the process of knowledge creation back on track. The following questions will help in the review process:

∎ Have we achieved the milestones along the road to developing a knowledge-creating organization?

∎ Do we need to develop some tools to measure success in knowledge creation?

∎ Can we develop more sophisticated knowledge audit tools?

The process of strategic planning for knowledge management and creation is messier than might be implied from the above categories. In reality, the strategic planning process is made up of non-linear feedback loops. As a result, the outcomes of the process can be unpredictable and may or may not be successful.

Knowledge-management drivers

Organizations have a number of potential levers at their disposal to aid their efforts in knowledge management. Most are straightforward, but they are often overlooked or neglected.

One of the main levers is the organization's customer database. Despite all the management literature on customer focus, many organizations still do not make enough of their customer information. In commercial organizations the major knowledge gap is often between the sales and marketing and the product development and manufacturing departments. Insufficient information is fed from the customers to the production areas and new products and services are starved of this feedback data. In education the knowledge gap is often between the pedagogic needs of students and the process of curriculum design, especially when the latter is in the hands of governmental agencies.

Educational institutions are very good at capturing what can be measured. Student, examination and other database knowledge is routinely collected in increasingly sophisticated information-management systems. The danger is that, as more explicit knowledge is catalogued and automated, other knowledge is filtered out. The big issue is how to lever the intangible assets to produce real benefits to students and create additional value.

People knowledge is, of course, one of the most valuable assets for any organization and a lever that is of the utmost importance. The management task is to create the climate and environment where people knowledge can best be used, shared and created. This organizational climate should also create organizational memory. Lessons that have been learnt need to be recorded and brought into play when new developments are being planned. Reinventing the wheel is something to be avoided at all costs.

If an organization is to take knowledge management forward, it needs to identify the drivers that can enhance the process.

Knowledge-management drivers:

■ integrate knowledge-management strategy into the overall aims of the organization;
■ communicate senior management commitment throughout the organization;
■ share knowledge effectively throughout the organization;
■ recognize the contribution that knowledge management makes to innovation;
■ recognize the contribution that knowledge management makes to customer loyalty;
■ improve staff capability for sharing knowledge and information;
■ maximize the organization's intellectual capital and knowledge assets;
■ establish a culture of lifelong learning;
■ recognize the contribution of knowledge management to organizational success.

Creating major change

A number of stages/phases are relevant if an organization is to be successful in the process of creating major change. John Kotter (1996) has identified an eight-stage process (*see below*). Amendments have been made to the process to reflect the requirements of knowledge management.

The implications for education

Despite the many examples in the business world, few educational institutions have risen to the challenge of developing strategies for knowledge management. Yet there is as much need for knowledge management in education as there is in business. If excellent results are achieved in one area of a school, college or university, there should be a process for knowing how they were achieved. Most importantly, there should be strategies in place to replicate that achievement elsewhere.

Establishing a sense of urgency	Conduct a knowledge audit Engage in scenario planning Identify the major threats and/or opportunities
Creating the guiding coalition	Get a group together who have enough influence to lead the change
Develop a vision and strategy	Create a knowledge vision Identify the steps necessary to implement that vision
Communicate the change vision	Use all possible channels to communicate the new vision and strategy – e-mail is just one Have organizational leaders as the role model for the desired behaviour, eg, sharing, creating and developing new knowledge
Empowering broad-based action	Get rid of the barriers to knowledge management and creation Change systems, such as intranets or other communication channels, that undermine the change vision Encourage the taking of risks in the creation and management of new knowledge
Generating short-term wins	Plan visible and immediate improvements in knowledge management or creation Reward individuals who have added to the knowledge stock of the organization
Consolidating gains and producing more changes	Use the change process to change other systems, policies and procedures, to ensure that they support the knowledge-management initiative Recruit and promote staff who will add value to the knowledge pool of the organization
Anchoring new approaches in the culture	Create better performance through knowledge management, leading to improved knowledge management Articulate the connections between knowledge management and organizational success

Educational institutions need to learn from the experience of consulting firms. The larger ones, such as Andersen Consulting and Ernst & Young, have recognized that they are selling know-how. They have made knowledge management a part of their mission and strategy. As they have grown and become global businesses, they have recognized the need to have mechanisms in place that enable them to share the enormous amount of expertise their consultants have developed. Such strategies require the sharing of both tacit and explicit knowledge, and sophisticated use of IT. They are central to the firms' business strategies and are as much about human resource policies as they are about technology. The knowledge-management strategy must not be isolated from the rest of the organization's strategy; it must be kept at the top of the agenda and integrated into developments in HR and IT.

The purpose of employing the techniques of scenario and strategic planning is to ensure that all staff have the benefit of the entire experience and information of their institution. (And the term 'institution' is intended to encompass all organizations – large, small, public and private – including educational institutions.) At one time, educationalists liked to see their work as separate from the business world. Today, they have to accept that education is subject to the same pressures of the marketplace, and that educational institutions need to perform just as well as any other organization. In recent years a wide range of business techniques, including performance management, quality assurance and total quality management, have had a direct or indirect impact on education, and knowledge management is set to do the same.

Knowledge management should have a resonance in education. One major function of education is the imparting of knowledge, and knowledge management looks at knowledge from a related perspective. Education ought to find it easier to embrace knowledge-management ideas, processes and techniques than many other organizations.

Why strategies sometimes fail

Knowledge-management strategies do have their pitfalls, and the development of a strategy by itself does not guarantee success. Average failure rates of knowledge-management initiatives can be between 20 and 50 per cent, with some researchers even putting the rate as high as 70 per cent. Researchers do agree, however, on the common mistakes that organizations make, which often constitute the reasons for failure.

The first mistake occurs when the knowledge-management strategy or programme is not mandated or initiated by senior management. Any project that does not have top-level commitment and support will fail. Lack of leadership kills most major cultural change projects stone dead. This is why it is a good idea to create a 'champion' role, such as chief knowledge officer (*see* page 41).

The second mistake occurs when knowledge-management programmes are driven by one department and not treated as a whole-organization initiative. A knowledge-management programme requires a coordinated effort between the IT and HR areas, but these two departments often do not communicate well. Employees' buy-in is as vital as technical solutions, and infrastructure needs to be linked with learning and training. In education, distinctions between curriculum and administration, or attempts to implement IT strategies in isolation, need to be avoided.

The third mistake is failing to involve staff sufficiently and obtain their buy-in to the initiative. According to the literature, a trend toward employee information-sharing is emerging. People responsible for certain business processes are now meeting to share and listen, in 'communities of practice' (*see* page 25). These communities can also share information with sister organizations that carry out similar work. It is important to remember that knowledge management is ultimately about people and must therefore start with them. This is an area where education may be well placed to go forward. Information-sharing and teamwork should be incorporated into staff performance reports and these should be used as the main motivators rather than financial incentives alone.

The fourth mistake occurs when knowledge management is seen as a quick fix rather than a sustained process. Successful use of knowledge-management tools and techniques requires a combination of culture change, organizational learning and process development, linked with technological solutions. It takes time to make the blend work. The danger in education is that such activities are often externally funded as projects, and 'projects' by definition have a finite life. The danger is that, once the project ends, so does the whole initiative.

A fifth mistake is to put too much emphasis on technology and too much faith in technological solutions. Intranets and document management are tools, not solutions. The vision needs to come first. Knowledge management will usually require and be linked to the IT strategy, but IT-centric approaches to knowledge management typically fail. Buying IT solutions will not guarantee success in knowledge creation.

Some reasons for failure

❚ Fear of change.
❚ Fear of failure.
❚ Too much faith in technical solutions.
❚ Assuming that it is a quick-fix solution, when it is actually a long-term process.

Some reasons for success

❚ Putting change in a cultural context.
❚ Employees buying in.
❚ Senior management leadership and commitment.
❚ Considering alternative scenarios.
❚ Producing a coherent strategy.

One of the major reasons why knowledge-management initiatives fail is because organizations consistently underestimate the fear among their staff of change and of the unknown. When new initiatives start, institutions can become awash with their own propaganda; the organizational ego-tripping is a delicate process. It is difficult to propel staff into the unknown, and to encourage them to adopt a new approach and attitude to their work. For this reason, a knowledge-management programme should be realistic. The process of scenario and strategic planning can help overcome the fear of change, but it is important to ensure that any strategy is capable of being delivered.

Over-ambition is a cause of many a failure. Pilot projects are a good means of learning the lessons before rolling out the full strategy. They can be useful to build up success before elaborate and costly programmes go institution-wide.

The ability to avoid failure and learn from mistakes is likely to be stronger when knowledge-management projects are attempted in institutions with shared visions and values. Such institutions usually engage in learning rather than indulging in blaming, and have a genuinely self-critical rather than a denial or compliant culture. Those who cannot honestly say that their culture is congruent with their values might do better to pay attention to cultural issues before striking out on the road to knowledge management. Building a learning culture is a good first step, because learning is the key to institutional self-knowledge.

5 Learning organizations

'The rate at which organizations learn may become the only sustainable source of competitive advantage.'

Peter Senge

Changes in information and communication technologies are having a profound effect on society and on the life of the people within it. Organizations need to build a culture of learning that allows for continuous knowledge creation and transformation. They need to understand how they create knowledge – that is to say, how they learn. This chapter concentrates on some of the key aspects of organizational learning and the links between learning, knowledge and creativity, and some of the techniques that can be employed to develop learning organizations.

Knowledge management and learning organizations

The concept of the learning organization is parallel to the concept of knowledge management. They are linked by the need to sustain a competitive advantage in a highly competitive world, by being able to innovate and adapt. Building a learning organization can be one of the most important activities for long-term organizational improvement and flexibility. The knowledge management gurus almost universally put enormous emphasis on the power of learning. Dorothy Leonard, for example, has argued that knowledge-based organizations are those that are enthusiastic about learning. They are continually learning and are consciously applying the results of that learning to their business. A learning culture is a key component for ensuring that an organization can benefit from the knowledge at its disposal.

John Burgoyne has also demonstrated the strong links between knowledge management and the learning organization. According to him, 'True knowledge management is about understanding and improving the way things work, how the different forms of knowledge can be linked, fed by organizational learning and used in adding value to goods and services' (1999). In arguing that tacit knowledge needs to be made explicit, Ikujiro Nonaka demonstrates that one major means of doing this is to ensure that a learning culture is established.

A learning organization encourages its staff to learn by giving them the mechanisms to share experience and best practice, and to improve their skills and capabilities. They have a knowledge-sharing culture, with knowledge as the 'cement' holding them together. The development of informal knowledge communities alongside more formal structures empowers staff to learn as they work, and builds a common language and context in which tacit knowledge, in particular, can be shared effectively. This allows the organization to build its knowledge and share best practices, and it can provide a link to strategy and reward systems.

Proclaiming the learning organization is not enough in itself. Important organizational changes and shifts in attitude and behaviour also have to take place. Reactive, fragmented and competitive structures will never provide fertile soil for organizational learning. There is a need to build the trust that allows people to share, and there is considerable evidence that organizations fail because they create a culture that inhibits trust and learning. Instead, organizations have to harness their core capabilities and competences, and develop strong knowledge communities, in which a systematic effort is made to build collaborative and sharing structures. This encourages staff to give commitment to the institution and its aims.

In *The Fifth Discipline*, Peter Senge wrote about how to create a learning organization, defined as one 'in which you cannot *not* learn because learning is so insinuated into the fabric of life'. He argues that there is a need to create structures 'where people continually expand their capacity to create the results they truly desire, where new and expansive thinking patterns are nurtured, where collective aspirations are set free, and where people are continually learning to learn together'.

Senge suggests a number of actions that organizations need to take to encourage organizational learning and to build a learning organization:

- adopt *systems thinking*, by integrating the other disciplines into a coherent body of theory and practice;
- encourage employees to take *personal mastery* of their own life;
- bring prevailing *mental models* to the fore and challenge them;
- build a *shared vision*;
- facilitate *team learning*.

The learning organization is a radically different concept from the traditional corporate training department. 'Learning organization' is not just another name for training, but describes a more holistic view of organizational learning. While formalized courses and training rooms have their place, a learning organization is a far wider and deeper concept. Action learning projects and other empowering forms of personal development are often used to challenge established views and work practices, and to build a culture of continuous learning.

Technology is an excellent tool for encouraging the development of a learning organization. Technological developments in broadcasting, ICT and communications, and the falling costs of its delivery, make it possible to offer staff access to a wide range of high-quality learning resources, either at their own desk or in a workplace learning centre. Online learning, video conferencing and CD ROMs all play their part, and new applications of information technology and digital broadcasting will open up even greater possibilities.

The concept of 'any time, any place, anywhere' is becoming increasingly important in learning organizations. It fits well into people's changed working patterns, but it is not entirely neutral. Lifelong learning can lead to an intensification of work – for example, many institutions give their staff laptop computers so that they can continue learning at home. While this sounds exciting and innovative, it can eat into people's personal time and space. Leatherwood (1999) has also argued that technological developments in learning of this type may reflect a masculine view of learning, and may restrict the opportunities available, or prevent some staff from embracing learning. Organizations need to ensure that learning opportunities are genuinely empowering.

A learning organization:

- has strong links to knowledge management;
- facilitates the development of a self-motivated and creative work-force;
- is more than the training department;
- promotes organizational learning;
- develops lifelong learning;
- involves all employees;
- liberates tacit knowledge;
- adds real value to the organization's activities.

Knowledge age intelligence

Traditional educational and testing processes

Chris Argyris has recognized one of the basic dilemmas of the knowledge age: 'Success in the marketplace increasingly depends upon people learning, yet most people do not know how to learn' (1998). Many organizations mistake IQ for the ability to learn. Unfortunately, employee competence was until comparatively recently linked closely to the notion of IQ, which treats intelligence in a narrow fashion. This in turn has led to very constrained ideas about learning. Learning has come to be seen as a rational pursuit in which notions of individual success figure prominently. Group learning is given little credence and the 'proper' sphere of learning is limited largely to the skills of verbal and logical reasoning. The knowledge age, however, requires people with far more diverse skills and competences. The core competences of the knowledge age include creative problem solving, innovation, the ability to work under pressure, and interpersonal, teamwork and leadership skills.

To cope with the new age of learning and the different forms of knowledge that exist within organizations, a new theory of intelligence is required. The theory of multiple intelligence put forward by Howard Gardner (1983) has had a considerable influence in education, and has important consequences for organizational learning.

Gardner has argued that traditional educational and testing processes have concentrated on too narrow a range of capabilities and ignore a wider range of human intelligence. Since the 1920s, psychologists have worked on measuring IQ, but limited it to certain skills. In particular, traditional IQ tests measure capability in the domains of verbal/linguistic and logical/

mathematical thinking. They leave out the social, personal and emotional skills that are essential to the way people function.

In the context of knowledge management, traditional IQ notions can be very restrictive. Organizations relying on this kind of assessment may be failing to recognize the full potential of their staff. Organizations need knowledge creation and this in turn requires a wide spread of capabilities.

Multiple intelligences

It is important for organizations to be able to use and develop the full range of human capabilities. Gardner has identified a number of separate strands to intelligence that encompass the whole of human capability. The first strand includes the ability to read, write and communicate with words – *verbal/linguistic* intelligence. The second strand is the ability to reason and think logically, and to use numbers to solve problems. While these are central components in the traditional IQ quotient, the difference is that for Gardner they are not the only forms of intelligence. He has also identified a number of additional important modes of intelligence:

- visual and spatial abilities, sometimes called *iconic*, which are about being able to draw, interpret diagrams and use maps;
- *musical ability*, closely related to the iconic;
- the *facility to use bodily movements skilfully*;
- *intrapersonal* intelligence, or the ability to understand oneself;
- the ability to understand other people, or *interpersonal* intelligence, which is closely related to intrapersonal intelligence.

More recently, Gardner has identified other types of intelligence, including the *naturalistic* (the ability to operate with phenomena in the natural world), as well as the *spiritual* and *existential* (the latter concerned with the way people are able to handle concerns about the nature of the human condition).

The theory of multiple intelligences has a considerable importance for knowledge management and for developing the creativity and innovation required in knowledge creation and transformation. Organizational activity was traditionally seen as rational-analytical, with decision making based on a fairly narrow range of competences, primarily logical and verbal/ linguistic. However, it is increasingly clear that the knowledge age demands a variety of styles of thinking and competences. Educationalists now realize that their system has too often written off people because of a too-narrow concept of intelligence; many other organizations are coming to the same conclusion.

Multiple intelligences (Gardner)

■ Verbal and linguistic intelligence.
■ Visual and spatial intelligence.
■ Musical intelligence.
■ Logical and mathematical intelligence.
■ Bodily and kinaesthetic intelligence.
■ Interpersonal (social) intelligence.
■ Intrapersonal intelligence.
■ Naturalistic intelligence (recognition of the environment and the natural world).
■ Existential intelligence (concern with the human condition).
■ Spiritual intelligence.

Emotional intelligence

Closely related to the idea of multiple intelligence is that of emotional intelligence. This idea, associated with John Mayer, Peter Salovey and Daniel Goleman, has developed considerable importance when judging the performance of managers and their ability to lead and to motivate people.

Teams and particularly knowledge communities work on the basis of good interpersonal relationships, and the ability of their members to empathize feelings and emotions. There is a recognition that teamwork makes a difference and creates more than individuals would do by themselves. This 'synergy' puts the 'buzz' into teamwork and is ideal for building knowledge-sharing communities, where crucially important intangible and tacit knowledge can be transferred. Successful team members and inspirational team leaders have some special characteristics. Among these are the interpersonal and intrapersonal intelligences identified by Gardner and what is now generally referred to as *emotional intelligence*.

Emotional intelligence subsumes Gardner's interpersonal and intrapersonal intelligences. The term refers to the ability to monitor one's own emotions and those of others, to discriminate among them, and to use the information to guide thinking and actions. Emotional intelligence involves abilities that Peter Salovey (1997) has categorized in five domains:

■ *Self-awareness* – knowing one's emotions and observing oneself and recognizing feelings as they occur. The ability to monitor and understand one's own emotions is of particular importance for self-understanding. Without it, people are at the mercy of their emotions.

▊ *Managing emotions* – handling feelings in such a way that they are appropriate in given situations; realizing what is behind such feelings as fears and anxieties, anger and sadness, and finding ways to handle them. People who have learnt how to manage their emotions often battle against distress. People who have this skill are able to bounce back from setbacks more easily.

▊ *Motivating oneself* – channelling emotions in the service of a goal, including emotional self-control, delaying gratification and stifling impulses. It is all about emotional control; people who are able to employ this intelligence tend to be more highly productive.

▊ *Empathy* – sensitivity to other people's feelings and concerns; taking their perspective and appreciating the differences in how people feel about things. Being able to recognize emotions in others is the most important 'people skill' and is essential in such occupations as sales, management, teaching and caring.

▊ *Handling relationships* – managing emotions in others, social competence and social skills. Essential for leadership and good interpersonal relationships and a key skill in managing organizations and being at ease in the social world.

These abilities bring intelligence to emotions and provide employees with the sensitivity to pick up tacit messages. (It is worth remembering that being good in one domain does not necessarily guarantee proficiency in others.)

Emotional intelligence is concerned primarily with right-brain characteristics such as imagination, feelings, emotions and creativity, instead of the logical-rational characteristics of the left brain. It helps people to work in teams and share their tacit knowledge. There is a strong link between excellent organizational performance and high levels of emotional intelligence among staff members. Building a high degree of social harmony is crucial for the flow of ideas, and for organizational success; team members need to feel easy with each other. Leading innovative teams requires superb leadership skills and an emotional intelligence that leads to trust in other people and a valuing of other people's ideas (however much they deviate from safe, corporate norms. Another aspect of this particular intelligence is an ability to cope calmly with pressure, even when the team's ideas or actions appear to threaten traditional authority.) Essentially, emotional intelligence is about important 'soft' skills and the ability to use people skills to enhance success.

Many organizations are now encouraging their employees to develop and explore their emotional intelligence, to express their feelings in a positive manner and to develop the creative side of their personality. Ideas and new thinking, or 'thinking out of the box' as it is sometimes called, are all encouraged, as are brainstorming, celebrating failure and generally being innovative.

The idea of multiple intelligences also has a considerable impact on the preferred learning styles of staff members when they are undertaking training or self-development. One of the best methods of knowledge-sharing is through training and development, but this will work only if staff enjoy the experience; this is more likely to occur if the style and methods of training match preferred learning styles.

The traditional bureaucratic approach to employee roles is vanishing as organizational structures change and become more democratic, participatory and open. Knowledge-based organizations have to pay attention to the particular intelligences they need to develop, and to the best methods of encouraging them. Successful knowledge management is closely linked to new ways of thinking and acting, and fresh ways of developing creative thought. If organizational success is all about developing new ideas, products and services, knowledge workers need different ways of thinking and need to have their full range of intelligences developed.

Difficult conversations

The value of emotional intelligence is its contribution to increased organizational and individual learning. One way that both emotional intelligence and learning can be enhanced is through the management of difficult and challenging issues.

Stone and his fellow authors (1999) have written about the art of difficult conversations. They show how properly managed challenging conversations can generate learning rather than conflict. They argue that difficult conversations often focus on making a point, and this is often the source of conflict. To move from conflict to learning in difficult conversations, it is necessary to engage in what are known as learning conversations. In order to generate learning rather than conflict, the emotions and interests of both parties need to be taken into account. From such a situation it is important to achieve a dialogue in which emotions are recognized, acknowledged and managed, and the implications for personal identity are explored.

We often forget how much learning happens through our normal life. It is often the difficult situations and out of the ordinary incidents that generate learning opportunities. But people can use these situations as learning opportunities only if they have the skills necessary to recognize them as such. A genuine learning dialogue can facilitate improved individual and organizational learning. A mechanism that allows difficult issues to be addressed openly and honestly creates a vehicle that allows tacit knowledge to be shared and made explicit. This may in turn lead not just to a better management of knowledge, but more importantly to the creation of new knowledge. In this respect, emotional intelligence is at the very core of knowledge management.

For learning conversations to be effective, it is necessary to do the following:

▮ sort out what happened;
▮ understand emotions;
▮ ground your identity;
▮ check your purpose;
▮ share your purpose;
▮ invite the other person to join as a partner in sorting out the situation;
▮ listen to understand;
▮ share your viewpoint;
▮ continually reframe;
▮ invent options;
▮ look to standards;
▮ talk about how to keep communication open.

Action learning – learning from what we do not know

Emotional intelligence and creative thinking are some of the main competences for the knowledge age, and action learning is a powerful means of delivering those competences and using them to best effect.

Action learning was originated by Reg Revans as both a philosophy and a method of learning. It is based on the notion that learning is not about recognizing what we know, but what we do *not* know. Revans developed his ideas while working as a coalfield manager during the Second World War. He found that traditional training techniques or bodies of knowledge did not solve the problems of the rapid change that was taking place in the coal industry. At such times, organizations that do not learn and make changes are doomed. Revans' approach was to develop action-learning teams, to ask questions and to generate new knowledge.

In Revans' formula for action learning, Learning = P+Q, where P stands for the traditional programme learning of books, seminars and lectures, and Q represents the learning that comes from questioning, sifting evidence and working in groups and teams. Learning is therefore a mix of the didactic and the experiential, but Revans' view is that action learning is primarily based on Q.

Action learning has been developed as an alternative to more traditional forms of learning in the classroom or the training suite, where learning is often deliberately isolated from real-life problems and situations. By contrast, action-learning programmes are centred upon practice. Participants learn by doing and through the act of being creative. They reflect upon the consequences of acting in particular and practical ways, and decide what works and what does not. Learning is done in real-life situations, by trying to solve real problems. The environment has to be one that encourages the sharing of any discoveries. The important point is that work is done on real problems and work is seen as a learning opportunity. It is a means of developing practical 'know-how' or tacit knowledge.

Projects in action learning

An interesting recent example of the type of creativity that action learning can generate is provided by 'Innovative ICT Projects in Irish Schools', supported by Ireland's schools integration project, 'Schools IT 2000'. Schools were encouraged to develop novel ICT solutions that were relevant to the needs of their pupils and the local community, and to do so in partnership with other schools and/or company sponsors. This was a bottom-up undertaking that deliberately used the action-learning approach.

A range of fascinating initiatives were developed, including 'The Sociology of Shopping', a cross-curricular project from a Dublin school that brought together aspects of geography, language, mathematics and history; 'Control Technology Empowering Minds', from another Dublin school, explored the use of control technology with primary children to open new gateways for learning; 'Euro-Opera: A collaborative European initiative in writing and producing a children's opera', from a school in Cork, was developed in partnership with industrial sponsors from six European countries; 'A Sense of Japan', also from a Cork school, focused on the lives of young Japanese people and sought to strengthen links between Eire, the European Union and Japan; and 'Open and Distance Learning for Circus and Fairground Families' was coordinated by a school in Limerick and supported by 18 other schools across Eire. All the projects demonstrate the power of the technique of action learning, and show how it can be used in education to inspire novel approaches to the curriculum.

Action learning in practice

Action learning usually involves small groups of participants working collectively to solve problems and to come up with novel solutions. These groups are known as *learning sets*. They may or may not have a facilitator or advisor. The sets often work best when they are interdisciplinary and are composed of people who are committed to making change happen.

Members of learning sets come together periodically to ask each other questions and to test each other's opinions and views. The purpose is to help them to reflect on what they have done and achieved, and to assist them in developing new approaches to problem solving. The learning that takes place is self-managed and usually project-based. It focuses on finding a solution internally without the use of external consultants, although good internal facilitation is essential. Developing an action plan, sharing it and submitting the plan to senior management completes the action-learning process.

Action learning is a method of unlocking the talents of the workforce, although its success depends on getting the right balance of reflection and action. It is a method by which tacit knowledge can be made explicit and is therefore susceptible to transmission throughout the organization. It can provide an excellent approach for organizational learning because its results are grounded in the activities and experiences of employees.

While action learning has been around for a considerable time, it is less widely used as a tool than it could be. Most organizations prefer to use structured training, concentrating on the topics and techniques that are considered to be valuable by management. Traditional training should not be decried, but much of it is wasted because it is not seen to be relevant to the task in hand. Action learning, on the other hand, has its basis in the reality of day-to-day issues and problems, and is specifically designed to be a problem-solving tool. Most importantly, it makes use of both the explicit and tacit knowledge that employees have of the situation and allows them an opportunity to contribute solutions and new ideas.

Action learning:

▌ is a means of making tacit knowledge explicit;
▌ is about learning from experience;
▌ is about learning in real situations to solve real problems;
▌ aids organizational learning and development;
▌ unlocks the talents of the workforce;
▌ is about making change happen.

Being creative

Closely aligned with action learning is a need in learning organizations to develop the techniques of creative thinking in employees. This is particularly important in organizations that wish to develop innovative management styles and find new and creative ways of working across existing organizational boundaries. The key word here is *creativity*. Being creative is a key skill in the knowledge age and one that all institutions need to inspire in their staff.

What does 'creativity' mean? What are the characteristics of creativity? It is an interesting phenomenon in the context of knowledge and knowledge management because being creative often has to do with what people *do not* know as much as with what they *do* know.

Creativity is about the novel and the new. It is about transforming situations and developing new ideas. Creativity is the ability to apply knowledge to solve problems and to innovate, and to be able to do this on a consistent basis. Creativity does not always involve new ideas. It can also be about transferring existing knowledge to new situations and putting it in different contexts. Or it can be about making connections in ways that have not been tried before. It is also possible to be creative and quite mistaken! A creative thought is not always a correct or a workable one, and one characteristic of creative people is their ability to tolerate mistakes, made either by themselves or by others.

While it can be an individual activity, creativity also needs to be explored in social and group settings. One important insight of social psychology is the way that creative synergy can occur when groups of people put their collective mind to solving problems. Creative people are usually very self-motivated. They positively want to solve problems and have an overwhelming desire to come up with fresh thinking. They find the very act of being creative both motivating and exhilarating. Creative people usually do not wait for others to define problems for them. Being creative requires high levels of emotional intelligence because creative individuals have high levels of self-assurance, good interpersonal skills, strong lateral-thinking skills, and the ability to work with others and to give – and take – criticism.

There is a popular misconception that you have to be a genius to be creative – someone like Einstein or Paul McCartney – but being creative can, in fact, be an everyday occurrence. The world is full of creative people. Creativity does not require particular levels of education or some superhuman intelligence. What it does require is the *context* in which it can flourish. Depending on the social setting, creativity can either be nurtured or frustrated. It is an active process, in which creative people construct new meaning, much of which is profoundly influenced by the situation in which the individual is located.

Creativity in organizations depends on the policies, attitudes, structures and culture of the workplace. Organizations can work on improving their staff's creative processes – but they will have to be prepared to manage the rush of new thinking that will be generated!

Developing creative thinking can be done experientially through activities of the action-learning type, or through more traditional training programmes, using techniques such as Edward de Bono's lateral and parallel thinking. Too often, thinking is not seen as a skill that can be learnt and developed, but as an attribute that people have in some measure. In fact, people can be taught to think, in the same way that they can be taught to do anything else. Staff are often expected to be creative without ever being given the right tools. Many of the tools, such as De Bono's six thinking hats (*see* page 24), are as simple and immediate as they are powerful. Yet a great deal of time is spent on aspects of training that do not push the organization forward, while powerful thinking tools are ignored. The thinking ability of employees is the key to developing new ideas and ways of working. They need to be able to 'think out of the box', to develop techniques and not just to tackle problems, but to test received ideas and to generate new ones in response to competition and changing client needs.

Recruiters in organizations often fail to focus on talent and creativity, but spend time instead on identifying work-related skills. These skills may have a limited life because of technological change. Many organizations put far too much emphasis on person or job specifications when recruiting. There is far too much predictability and a 'safety first' attitude to recruiting. Recruitment needs to look instead at whether a person can solve problems, or develop new ideas or new ways of doing things.

Creativity is strongly related to organizational culture. It is not good enough for organizations to recruit people with creative potential and expect them to keep coming up with the goods. Creativity needs the right environment if it is to thrive. Encouraging creativity means ensuring that the organizational culture, structures and processes are right. The right teamwork, the right leadership and the right projects for people to work on, which will stretch and use their talents to the full, are essential. Creative people thrive on challenges and their work needs to provide them with the opportunities to use their capacity for innovation.

Organizational structures can strangle as well as enhance creativity. It is difficult to think and to be creative in a culture of blame and distrust, and it is impossible to be creative where there is rigidity of thought. Creative people need the right social context in which to develop their ideas. They also need guides and mentors and other creative people to bounce ideas off. Learning and creativity are social constructs built up through shared exchange, collaboration and, often, group work. The ethos and leadership styles within organizations may have to be changed if new thinking and creativity are to be encouraged.

Creativity:

▌ is about novel ways of thinking;
▌ is about making connections that have not been made before;
▌ is about transforming situations;
▌ is about transferring knowledge to different contexts;
▌ is about solving problems;
▌ is about self-motivation;
▌ is not related to traditional notions of intelligence;
▌ can be an individual or a group activity;
▌ is strongly related to organizational culture, which can encourage or strangle it.

E-learning

The exponential growth of the Internet is having a dramatic impact on learning. Until recently, the growth has been in business-to-business and business-to-consumer transactions. However, the development of online learning means that learner-to-education transactions will soon be the third main strand in Internet traffic. The World Bank has estimated that by the year 2020, around 90 million students will be taking degrees or shorter qualifications via distance learning; the market of this area of education could soon be worth more than $100 billion worldwide. According to John Chambers, Chief Executive Officer of Cisco Systems, 'The next big killer application for the Internet is going to be education. Education over the Internet is going to be so big, it's going to make e-mail usage look like a rounding error'.

What is *e-learning* and what impact will it have on the way people learn and take up education? It is interesting that the term is 'e-learning' and not 'e-education'. This shows that much of the online learning in the future will be self-learning rather than institution-based. There are a number of definitions of e-learning, but Marc Rosenberg (2001) defines it usefully as follows:

The use of the Internet to deliver a broad array of solutions that enhance knowledge and performance. It is based on three fundamental criteria: e-learning is networked, which makes it capable of instant updating, storage/retrieval/distribution and sharing instruction or information; it is delivered to the end-user via a computer using standard information technology; it focuses on the broadest view of learning – learning solutions that go beyond the traditional paradigms of training.

Technology-based training has been around for many years, but the Internet and its linked technologies have given it an enormous boost in terms of speed, immediacy and in interaction between learners and instructors. The fact that it is easy to update has enormous implications for lifelong learning and in-company training (where training can be delivered via corporate Intranet). The London *Financial Times* predicted in April 2000 that, by 2003, 30 per cent of all learning will be delivered over corporate Intranets.

The increase in e-learning is driven by the business benefits that can be provided through learning on an Intranet or via the Internet. Rosenberg believes that the benefits are significant and can include the following:

- lower costs;
- enhanced business responsiveness;
- messages that are consistent or customized depending on need;
- timely or dependable content;
- learning can be 24 hours a day and 7 days a week;
- no 'ramp up time';
- universality;
- the build-up of community;
- scaleability;
- the leverage of corporate investment on the Web;
- the provision of an increasingly valuable customer service.

The changing patterns of learning will offer threats as well as opportunities to traditional educators, and new paradigms for them to cope with. The online learning world is not open to traditional educators by right. Many of the organizations exploiting online learning are new to the business, and do not hold the same attitudes or have the same structures as traditional educational institutions. The new entrants recognize that the new markets for education and learning are global and universal, while most educational institutions have traditionally seen themselves operating within local geographical catchments. This could lead to considerable competition in areas where, often, none existed before.

However, it is not just the structures of education that are under threat from e-learning. The very nature of learning is being changed by technology. Technology makes the learning experience more personal and interactive. In *Growing Up Digital*, Don Tapscott described the shift to interactive learning as a move from the traditional one-size-fits-all learning to a new lifelong learning culture that is customized to the individual learner. Tapscott argues that traditional approaches to learning have been linear. Whether using lectures, seminars, books or instructional videos, learners start from the beginning and work to the end. Tapscott believes that the Internet is different because learners surf it in an interactive and non-linear fashion.

ICT in education can accelerate creativity, providing a medium for thinking differently. Hyperlinks and information sources can be navigated at any point. Such non-linear learning allows more learner-centred and customized learning than has previously been possible. It also allows the learner to take control over his or her own learning. These changes have enormous implications for education. In the knowledge age, new paradigms will open up for learning, and new and different institutional forms will emerge to deliver it.

Shifting to interactive e-learning

- Hypermedia learning as opposed to linear, sequential learning.
- Construction/discovery as opposed to instruction.
- Learner-centred as opposed to teacher-centred.
- Learning how to learn, as opposed to absorbing materials.
- Lifelong learning as opposed to institution-based learning.
- Customized as opposed to one-size-fits-all.
- School as fun as opposed to school as torture.
- Teacher as facilitator as opposed to teacher as transmitter.

Corporate universities

One of the most interesting of the relative newcomers to the education scene is the corporate university, which has taken the concept of the learning organization a stage further, and formalized it.

A corporate university is an in-house education and training facility, which addresses the particular learning needs of an organization. Companies that have already established them realize that they gain a competitive advantage from developing wide-ranging organizational learning and a sophisticated range of learning tools. Corporate universities differ from traditional company training departments for the following reasons:

- they fulfil a far wider strategic role;
- they usually have a role in training employees from supply-chain and customer companies as well as staff from the parent organization;
- they have generally developed a strong range of training in core competences;
- they are major vehicles for transmitting organizational values and culture;
- they often have links with traditional universities, who may accredit aspects of their programmes.

Corporate universities have developed quickly in such companies as British Aerospace and the Lloyds TSB bank, and worldwide there may now be as many as 2,000 such universities. Within the companies that have developed them there is a recognition that training is not a cost but an investment. Substantial employee development is vital if the company is to attract and retain the best people in the workforce. The corporate university is an example of a company taking responsibility for its own employee development.

In her book *Corporate Universities* (1998), Jeanne Meister describes the shift that is taking place from education and training to the 21st-century paradigm of *learning*. She goes on to show how companies are using the shift to design their own in-house corporate universities. This shift has opened up the debate on lifelong learning and made employee development a hot topic. The move to provide opportunities for continuous professional development means that reliance on external training programmes is often insufficient. There is a real competitive advantage to be gained from having an in-house corporate university, as employers who offer such facilities will be seen as employers of choice by the brightest and most creative jobseekers.

Jeanne Meister views the corporate university as a portal within a company through which all education is delivered. The portal provides the strategic hub for educating both internal and external stakeholders and links an organization's strategies to the learning goals of its audiences. The corporate university highlights the importance to business of lifelong learning, and helps employees to recognize the need for a lifetime commitment to self-development. In the corporate university, they are encouraged to change their thinking and to improve their skills to meet the new global marketplace.

Some argue that corporate universities may take over from traditional universities as the primary institutions of lifelong learning, displacing their monopoly. Indeed, in the United States, the number of corporate universities may soon exceed the number of traditional institutions. Some corporate universities are already going head-to-head with traditional universities by offering courses to the general public as well as to their own staff. This of course gives everyone a wider choice and makes education an increasingly competitive marketplace.

However, while corporate universities can be a threat, they can also present opportunities for higher education. Many traditional institutions are already involved in collaborative partnerships with corporate universities, sharing libraries, laboratories and research, and validating customized degree programmes. Such collaborations can bring considerable (and much-needed) financial benefits too. However, such a collaboration will work only if the traditional institutions can move from their 'one-size-fits-all' philosophy of education, and develop more customized products to satisfy the corporate needs and culture of their private partners. Developing particular specialisms for niche markets is one way of providing added value to a corporate university.

Corporate universities:

▮ provide an in-company approach to knowledge creation;
▮ are more than traditional training departments;
▮ may have strong links to traditional universities;
▮ may start rivalling traditional universities;
▮ have pioneered new methods of learning;
▮ can be an important means of developing a learning organization.

The implications for education – developing creative learning

Notions of education and learning

In the knowledge age, education is about learning, creativity and thinking. Yet these topics are rarely on the curriculum and are not usually taught as subjects in their own right. Students are very infrequently provided with the tools with which to think or to be creative. Too often education, particularly the traditional examination curriculum, is based on students being able to replicate 'model' answers, rather than being rewarded for coming up with novel solutions. In *Living on Thin Air*, Charles Leadbetter argues that educational systems will need to move from the chronological model of education to one that is based on creativity, collaboration and learning how to learn.

Education and learning continue to be seen as the province of the few, and education is still primarily institutionally-driven, with success or failure as the end point of any learning experience. While qualifications are important, it is vital to find ways to divorce the notion of learning from assessment. Notions of fixed intelligence, and what it means to be educated and clever, still abound and culture still divides society into 'the educated' and 'the others'. Learning has yet to develop a populist focus in the way that medical issues, for example, have been popularized by the health, fitness and diet movement. Learning needs to be covered in popular magazines in the same way that health and fitness are. While the lifelong learning revolution has moved the debate forward, too many people still associate education with social exclusivity and power. This important issue of cultural change needs to be dealt with. Human talent and resources are being wasted, or directed into uncreative areas; people are unable to discover the full range of their talents and are missing out on the joys of learning.

One of the key themes to emerge in recent years is the recognition that learning is not an event that occurs only at the beginning of life. Instead, it is a lifelong activity. Throughout the journey, learning may take many forms and be delivered in many different ways. While the late 19th- and 20th-century paradigm held that the state was responsible for education, the 21st-century notion is that individuals have responsibility for their own personal development and their own learning.

Education is still insufficiently flexible. In the industrial economy of the past, when only a small minority of the population went into occupations that required high levels of literacy, the traditional academic curriculum may have made sense as the main educational route. Today, knowledge and lifelong learning are key issues, and the curriculum needs to be subjected to root-and-branch change, with the emphasis on developing creativity. Education may have made people think, but it did not necessarily teach them *how* to think, or provide thinking skills. Education has often used too narrow a definition of learning, based on a restrictive model of intelligence, concerned largely with academic ability. Consideration has also been given to the synergy between work, innovation and learning. This narrow model of learning filters out some of the most important intelligences and abilities. It ignores the relationship between work and learning, and the relationship between work and learning and change and creativity.

Education is a catalyst for change, particularly in respect of developing new ways of earning a living. The workplace is rarely thought of as a place of learning – a laboratory where people can develop new skills and capabilities – but it is essential now to find new ways of linking the workplace into the mainstream of learning.

The knowledge age requires a heterogeneous approach to developing the core competences that are required. Education policy-makers need to tackle a number of key issues. Education itself has to change, and to develop new models, concepts and frameworks. Scenarios should be drawn up, speculating about what the world will be like in 2010, 2020 or even 2050. What will people need to know, and what is the best way for them to learn it? If this shift in thinking is not made, education will be seriously out of step with the need for creativity in the workplace, and will be filtering creativity out rather than building it in.

Learning and creativity

The knowledge age requires broader definitions of learning. *Learning in practice* needs to be favoured over abstract notions of learning. This approach allows learning to be fluid and linked to the interests and concerns of people, and to be relevant to their life and interests. It develops the motivation for learning by making it relevant to individual practice. It provides a bridge between work and learning. The link is the development of *learning communities*, who use action learning (*see* page 24) to build creativity. Such *situational learning* allows people to hold learning conversations (*see* page 18), where they solve problems, tell *stories* and share insights, from hunches and feelings to analysis and well-researched ideas. The motivation so essential for creativity is harnessed, coming from the fact that the learning has meaning to each individual because it becomes a part of their identity. The learners construct meaning through their interactions in a learning community.

The employer has the responsibility to create the conditions in which learning communities can flourish. They need to create the teams, put in the staff development and ensure that their staff have the training to make the most of the opportunities. The responsibility of the education system is to recognize these trends and develop creativity as a major theme in the curriculum. Clearly, creativity will be a key theme for learning in the 21st century.

In *The Creative Age: Knowledge and skills for the new economy* (2001), Kimberley Seltzer and Tom Bentley discuss the implications for education of the creativity required for the new knowledge-based economy. They categorize a number of characteristics that the new creative learners need to have:

- the ability to identify problems rather than depending on others to define them;
- the ability to transfer knowledge gained in one context to solve problems in another;
- the capacity to focus attention on the pursuit of a goal, or a set of goals; and
- the belief in learning as an incremental process, in which repeated attempts will eventually lead to success.

Educational processes will need to be designed to provide the opportunities for the development of these essential creativity skills. Drawing upon a range of international case studies from the United States, Canada and Sweden, Seltzer and Bentley identify a number of key characteristics of learning environments that encourage creativity (these apply to both educational and corporate environments):

- *trust* – secure, trusting relationships are essential if people are to take risks and learn from their failures;
- *freedom of action* – the creative application of knowledge is only possible where people are able to make real choices over what they do and how they are able to do it;
- *variation of context* – the experience that learners need when applying their skills in a range of contexts in order to make connections between them;
- *the right balance between skills and challenge* – creativity emerges in environments where people are engaged in challenging activities and have the right level of skills to meet them;
- *interactive exchange of knowledge and ideas* – creativity is fostered in environments where ideas, feedback and evaluation are constantly exchanged and where learners can draw on diverse sources of information and expertise;
- *real-world outcomes* – creative ability and motivation are reinforced by the experience of making an impact, achieving outcomes and changing the way things are done.

In order to bring about greater creativity in educators at all levels, including administrators, teachers and principals, local and national policy-makers will need to reflect on the nature of the curriculum, learning processes, learning infrastructures, career patterns, financial rewards for educators and the links between the community and educational organizations. It will not be easy, but the price will be high if no attempt is made to learn from experience.

New technology will force educational institutions to engage in a deep reflection and analysis about the whole process of teaching and learning. It has the capacity to facilitate highly customized learning opportunities for individuals. At the same time, educational institutions will want to preserve the sense of community and belonging that is so often at the core of a learning environment.

The impact of technology and the power of the Internet and e-learning will need to be modelled. In any future scenario, education needs to help all individuals to maximize multiple intelligence. Corporate universities will have an important role to play and will introduce new and exciting concepts of learning, particularly in the workplace. New ideas such as e-learning, collaborative learning, learning portals and so called 'skill-snacks' will develop alongside action learning approaches.

6 Bridging the digital divide

'People lack many things: jobs, shelter, food, health care and drinkable water. Today, being cut off from basic telecommunications services is a hardship almost as acute as these deprivations, and may indeed reduce the chances of finding remedies to them.'

Kofi Annan, United Nations Secretary-General

The knowledge age is one of the greatest periods of innovation and creation in history. It is changing the way we think about receiving and using information and processing knowledge. The revolution in telecommunications is creating unprecedented change in communications, finance, new jobs and access to global markets. It is changing approaches to global business practices as well as creating new notions of community. It demands new ways of thinking, new ways of working and new ways of learning. Education will be transformed by technology in the next 10 years. The technology needs to be mastered, but we also need to be able to use and apply the vast amounts of information that it makes available. This gives educators the challenge of identifying what knowledge is most useful. Technology also throws up the challenge of social inclusion. This chapter focuses on one of the biggest problems the knowledge age has – how to overcome the digital divide and create a digitally inclusive society.

Technology – a driver and a divider

While managing knowledge is not prefaced on new technology, new technology is clearly one of its major drivers. It is changing the context of how organizations communicate, as well as fundamentally altering the nature of their core business. It is, therefore, crucial as an indicator of the pace of change to look at how individuals, organizations and indeed nations are gearing up to the knowledge age. Being comfortable with new technology is a prerequisite of the knowledge age, in the same way that a reasonable standard of literacy was in the industrial age.

The digital revolution has introduced the world to e-commerce, text messaging, online shopping, online entertainment and e-mail, will doubtless bring other innovations including e-government and digital democracy, and will soon make mass online learning a reality. But despite the immense changes in technology, we do not inhabit a totally digital world. In the year 2000, Cisco Systems released TV advertisements showing people in the developing world entering the Internet age with the words 'Are you ready?' One year on, the majority of the world's population have never heard of the Internet and even fewer have used it – hardly surprising, in view of the statistic that some 80 per cent of the world's population have never even used a telephone. The Internet is not a part of the world for the majority and the technology is still out of reach for very many people, both in the developed and the developing world. While technology is an enormous force for bringing people together, it is also a divider:

> *The most widely feared prediction surrounding the digital revolution is that it will splinter society into a race of information haves and have-nots, knowers and know-nots, doers and do-nots – a digital divide. This revolution holds the promise of improving the lives of citizens but also the threat of dividing us. (Don Tapscott 1996)*

In society, one group of people have the best computers, access to the Internet, fast telephone services, and the education and opportunities to make effective use of what technology can offer. But it is the other group, the people who stand outside the information economy, who are the majority. Principally, but not exclusively, they are the poor, the unemployed, the low-skilled, and those on low incomes. They often have a limited educational background and a poor command of their own language. They are either reluctant or do not have the resources to join the digital age. The term 'digital divide' describes the gap between those who have access to and can effectively use the new information and digital technology, and those who do not and cannot. It is a key issue of the knowledge age, if not *the* key issue.

Those who do not have access to technology find themselves at a severe disadvantage. Being on the wrong side of the divide means fewer opportunities to take part in the information economy, and to take advantage of the educational, training, shopping, entertainment, financial, business and communications possibilities that are increasingly available. It threatens to cut them off from jobs and prosperity, and exclude them from participating in their society; for many, it can lead to even greater isolation. It also potentially starves the new-economy employers of the skilled employees they need. The divide may also separate digitally competent children from their digitally illiterate parents.

Once they are on the wrong side of the divide, some people may be stuck there for life. This provides educators worldwide with one of their major challenges – the ability to transform this divide into a digital opportunity and to bring about digital inclusiveness and to ensure that all people have the skills for the digital economy.

The worldwide digital divide

In the developing world

The digital divide is one of the most important social and political issues arising from the use of the Internet and the development of new technology, and an important one for political leaders worldwide. In the UK, New Labour has made certain promises about online development, and it was an important domestic issue for the Clinton administration. The United Nations has also put it somewhere near the top of its agenda. At Telecoms 99, the UN Secretary-General warned of the dangers of excluding the bulk of the world's population from the information revolution.

Today, some 15–20 per cent of the world's population is online. On the face of it, this sounds very positive for a relatively new invention, but half of these users are in the world's richest economy, the United States. By August 2000, it was estimated that there were over 116 million US online subscribers. The UK has about 15 million subscribers. By contrast, Africa, with a population of 740 million, has just one million Internet users. One of the reasons for this gap is poverty, but Africa's lack of modern telecommunications infrastructures is equally significant. Only 14 million people (less than the population of Tokyo) have phone lines on the whole of the African continent, and 80 per cent of those lines are in six of the continent's leading economies.

Like the UN, the World Bank believes that access to information technology will be the determining factor for successful and sustainable development for communities in the 21st century. Critics argue that there are more pressing needs for less well-off countries, but there is a strong argument that access to technology will help to bridge the wealth gap. The challenge is not only to provide the necessary technological tools but also to make those tools work for the achievement of economic, social and political change.

The problem is not limited to access to computers. The digital divide can only be bridged if the *connectivity* divide is bridged. The continuing lack of technological advance in certain countries is often blamed on monopolistic telephone operators, as well as on the prohibitive cost of laying down the necessary infrastructure. Governments around the world often own and control their country's telecom system, and high prices and poor service can lead to low take-up and access, especially by the less well-off sections of the community. And, as well as being related to telecommunications infrastructures, technological advance in developing countries is also about security, regulation, protection of foreign investment and the question of whether trickle-down economics works.

Even where there is an adequate telecommunications infrastructure, and the other issues are resolved, illiteracy and a lack of computer skills exclude many people from access to technology and the Internet. This aspect of the divide is usually linked to a lack of education and poverty. And in those parts of the world where English is not the mother tongue, a lack of English is a definite barrier; the Internet is still overwhelmingly dominated by this language.

The gap between the global information haves and the digital have-nots is widening, for the following reasons:

▌ poverty;
▌ lack of a (suitable) telecommunications infrastructure – the connectivity divide;
▌ lack of an electricity supply infrastructure;
▌ remote and rural locations;
▌ illiteracy and lack of basic skills;
▌ cost and availability of computers;
▌ lack of computer skills;
▌ poor educational infrastructures;
▌ lack of knowledge of the English language;
▌ an inability to see digital technology as applicable to everyday life.

There is fierce discussion about the digital divide and the priorities of international aid. Some argue that many issues should be prioritized way before IT developments. Surely sanitation, hygiene, health care and safe drinking water are more important than access to information and knowledge? In Africa, where there is an AIDS pandemic, why should anyone worry that only a tiny percentage of the population can surf the Internet? Famously, Microsoft founder Bill Gates has entered the debate by saying that the developing world has little need for computers; at a major conference in Seattle in October 2000, he asserted that 'the world's poorest two billion desperately need health care, not laptops'. However, others support the opposite view. Many believe that the poverty gap is already too great, and that allowing the IT gap to widen will only add to the difficulties of the developing world.

The counter-argument contends that computers and the Internet can have a huge transforming effect on developing economies. There is no one reason to deploy the technology. They can provide an enormous boost to traditional industry by making access to the world market easier. For example, an Internet service in rural India, called TARAhaat.com, has been designed to meet the needs of rural villagers. The technology allows users to record statistics about land, seed and machinery, to look up information about health clinics and jobs, to find buyers for crops and handicrafts, and to shop for household items. In Bangladesh, GrameenPhone is using demand aggregation to provide commercial phone services to poor rural villages. Such initiatives are not primarily about technology; they are about giving people choices and the opportunity to transform their lives by skipping directly to the digital world and joining the global economy. Elsewhere in India, technology is used to maximize the rich pool of indigenous talent and slow down the 'brain drain' to places such as Silicon Valley.

Tele-medicine is one of the main potential benefits of new technology. In the UK, it is set to become a reality by 2005, providing a wide range of services and improving access to medical expertise for patients, GPs and ambulance workers. In developing countries, the Internet can transform health care by providing access to health information and medical knowhow that could never be available locally. Remote communities with little chance of having their own health clinic or hospital service could have online access to medical advice and services. Educational opportunities could be improved in a similar fashion, with distance learning available online for remote communities. The Internet can make learning a reality for millions who would otherwise never have the opportunity of schooling or higher education.

A number of major companies, including Cisco Systems, IBM, HP and Anderson Consulting, are putting money into a variety of e-projects in the developing world. The UN initiative 'Digital Opportunities Task Force', or 'dot.force', is endorsed by many of the world's major economic powers.

This, and other initiatives, including Cisco's netaid.org, Hewlett Packard's Digital Village Program, and the UN's Development Programme (UNDP), are based on the belief that expanding access to digital technology can play a crucial role in the development of poorer economies.

In the developed world

The digital divide, or *e-exclusion*, is not just an issue for the less-developed countries of the world. It exists even in wealthy economies. Using Internet access as a proxy for computer skills, we find in the UK that, while the amount of Internet usage has increased among the poorer sections of the population, the rate of usage is lower than in wealthier sections, and the divide is growing. Of the poorest households, just 3 per cent have access to the Internet, while 48 per cent of the richest household are online. Increasingly, middle-income households are getting online, but the largest increase in 2001 is from wealthy households. There is also a rural/urban divide, with members of poorer remote communities using the Internet least, even though it could potentially benefit them most.

The digital divide is a major issue in British domestic social policy. The British Irish Council, for example, has identified the knowledge economy and the problems of the digital divide as major priorities for member administrations. In the year 2000, Ireland's Information Society Commission published a report entitled 'How the General Public is adapting to the Information Society in Ireland'. It found that 54 per cent of the adult population was familiar with PCs, and 43 per cent were familiar with the Internet; 41 per cent of the adult population had access to the Internet and a further 36 per cent had access to e-mail, with 47 per cent having access to a PC or laptop computer. Interestingly, 95 per cent of people surveyed believed that within the next 10 years all schoolchildren would be using computers as part of their education, and 88 per cent believed that school-children will need to be familiar with information and communications technologies to get a job. Although Ireland is a society that has made a positive commitment to becoming an information society, it still faces some considerable challenges. Of the population not in work, only 30 per cent were familiar with PCs as opposed to 87 per cent of students. Preparedness for the information society is at its highest among the young, urban middle classes. The divide is at its widest among the poor, the unemployed and those living in remote and rural communities. This is a pattern repeated elsewhere in the developed world.

Members of the European Union demonstrate varying rates of Internet penetration. In 2001, Sweden had a penetration rate of over 50 per cent, compared with 35 per cent in Germany and the UK. Spain's rate of 15 per cent shows how far some nations have to go to catch up with the leaders. The figures are important as proxies for skills in the knowledge age.

The EU has a range of strategies for jobs in the information age. At the 2000 Lisbon European Council, the goal was set for Europe to become 'the most competitive and dynamic knowledge-based economy in the world, capable of sustainable economic growth with more and better jobs and greater social cohesion'. Interestingly, the EU strategy is linked to lifelong learning and particularly e-learning, and sets specific IT targets for schools. By the end of 2001, the aim is for all schools in member countries to be connected to the Internet. In the employment field, all jobs will have to adapt to the knowledge age and one of the targets is digital literacy for all workers.

The digital divide largely mirrors the learning divisions in society. Despite the increasing numbers of young people and adults studying in both further and higher education, and the expanding opportunities for learning at work, there are still major differences in access and a lack of opportunities for people in the lower socio-economic groups. Those who have left education early and have few skills are at the lower ends of the work and pay hierarchies, and they generally enjoy fewer formal opportunities for learning through their employment.

There is a considerable and worrying learning divide in the workplace as well. On the one hand, there are those who are already well educated and who will continue to be lifelong learners. On the other, there are those who leave education largely unqualified and who do not engage in learning as adults and have little intention of doing so in the future. The Kennedy Report on widening participation in further education confirms this divide. In her report for the Further Education Funding Council in England, Baroness Helena Kennedy reported that the success of recent policies to increase participation and achievement in learning had been 'mainly in providing opportunities for those who have already achieved or continue to do so!'. If people are alienated from learning in general it is less likely that they will be motivated to develop digital skills.

The problems of access to information technology are often linked with basic skill issues of literacy and use of numbers (although many educators have found IT to be an excellent vehicle to help people develop basic skills). According to Ursula Howard (2000), delivering basic skills via IT has advantages over traditional methods, not only because it is seen as non-judgemental, but also because learners will be using the same technology as people acquiring much higher levels of skill. As she puts it, 'IT empowers the basic-skills learners; mainstreams the learning purpose; enables people to focus on their core purposes for learning' (2000). The digital divide is a symptom of a greater learning divide that needs to be tackled in parallel.

But it is not only exclusion *from* information that is a problem. It may be, as Perri 6 and Ben Jupp (2001) have argued, that exclusion *by* information is the greater problem. Their point is that the rise of the knowledge economy means that a large section of the population is increasingly excluded from basic services and opportunities provided by both governmental and business organizations, on the grounds that they constitute bad risks.

In recent years, a number of initiatives have been used to overcome this divide. The main focus of government action in the UK, Europe and North America has been to improve the *supply side* of learning, to provide more access to equipment and to get large sections of the population connected. More recently, there has been parallel action to develop skills and the demand for learning. In the UK, this has included the establishment of the University of Industry, the National Grid for Learning and government encouragement to further education colleges to increase their access to people on the other side of the divide. In 2000, David Blunkett, then Secretary of State for Education and Employment, launched a National E-Learning Foundation. The foundation aims to provide access to laptops for all schoolchildren, especially those from the most deprived backgrounds. If successful, this will bring a computer into the home of the people who are least likely to purchase one for themselves.

In Scotland in January 2001, Deputy Social Justice Minister Margaret Curran announced the establishment of new community cyber-cafés, to encourage local people to explore new technology and show how it can make a positive impact on their daily life, from shopping to learning. There will also be a £1.5 million network of eight *digital champions* across Scotland, who will help develop other ICT projects in hard-pressed communities. Digital champions will work to improve ICT provision in social-inclusion partnership areas, advising and helping with start-ups, accessing funding, engaging the private sector and spreading best practice.

The UK government's Communications White Paper, published in 2000, has made a commitment to universal Internet access by 2005. The increase is likely to accompany the switch to digital television, which will bring e-mail and interactive programming into homes that currently do not have computers. In addition, there will be considerable increases in the number of devices that can access the Internet, including 3G mobile phones.

Despite all these developments, there is a word of warning here. Although access is a key issue, it does not necessarily guarantee that it will be used, or used in such a way that people will learn new skills or develop computer literacy. Increased access needs to be complemented by a process to encourage learning so that it can lead to real skills and learning revolutions.

The United States is grappling with the same issues. Despite the highest standard of living and the highest Internet access in the world, it still has an immense gulf between digital haves and have-nots. The 'Falling Through the Net' series of reports, published by the National Telecommunications and Information Administration (NTLA), graphically illustrates the problems. The administration has put forward a number of solutions. The reports show how quickly Internet access has grown in the United States and the importance that it has to the economy. However, they also show that there is a much lower than average take-up by minority groups, principally Hispanics, Blacks, Pacific Islanders and Asian-Americans, and also by people with a range of disabilities, particularly those with a hearing impairment and problems with their manual dexterity. 'Falling Through the Net' points out that Hispanic-Americans are only half as likely as their White counterparts to own a computer and are 2.5 times less likely to use the Internet. US Secretary of State Colin Powell is reported to have said, 'If the digital divide persists, we all lose. The digital have-nots will be the poorer, more resentful of progress than ever and will not be able to become the skilled workers or potential customers that are needed to sustain the growth of the Internet economy.'

Causes of the digital divide in the developed world

- Poor educational background and lack of basic skills.
- Lack of computer skills.
- Low incomes and poverty.
- Lack of access to digital technology.
- Social and ethnic background.
- Cost of computers.
- High telephone charges.
- Perceived lack of relevance to people's lives.

The institutional divide

The digital divide is not just an international and domestic social issue. The gap between the digitally literate and the rest is a problem for all organizations. Companies, and voluntary, public and educational bodies all suffer equally from a skills gap in their workforce. In the knowledge age, all organizations need their staff to have digital skills. Ensuring that all staff can use and gain value from digital technology and seize its potential is a colossal task, particularly for older and less well-educated staff.

Many institutions are experimenting with a range of initiatives to deal with the problem and many have made it a central theme of their training and lifelong-learning policies. Training and learning centres in organizations are part of the answer, although a corporate strategy to put everyone online is the key to reducing the divide. The real problem is that not enough organizations have seen the advantage that can be gained from doing business online, or in using technology to improve their knowledge-management processes. There is a considerable digital advantage to be gained from recognizing the impact that technology can have, and in using it effectively.

In workplace training the use of ICT needs to be seen as a major feature of professional development. And it is not just software skills that need to be taught; all staff need to learn the essentials of how to communicate internally and externally, and how to use technology to build up communities of practice.

Causes of the digital divide in organizations

- Organizational policies that do not take advantage of the digital age.
- Lack of skills among staff.
- Lack of investment in training.
- Lack of access to the Internet.
- Lack of motivation to use the new technologies.
- The age of staff.
- Lack of organizational knowledge-management policy.

Lessons for education – delivering the knowledge dividend

The key to delivering the digital dividend lies with education (prefaced on the appropriate telecommunications infrastructure being in place). The report from the second CKO Summit, held at Luttrellstown Castle in Dublin, points out the following:

To date, little attention has been given to the teaching of information literacy skills. The lack of these skills is a real roadblock to the development of the knowledge economy and to the realization of the benefits of the knowledge economy. (1999)

When we talk about skills we need to make a distinction between the requirements of early and late adopters of IT. The characteristics of each tell us a great deal about social divisions in society and about those groups where the digital age is having its greatest impact. What distinguishes the early adopters from the late adopters? Are there characteristics that distinguish those who see new technology as a boon from those for whom it holds little or no interest, or who are frightened by it?

In its report 'Information Society Ireland' (2000), the Irish Information Society Commission analysed the two groups. According to them, it is generally individuals and communities experiencing social exclusion in society who are most at risk from exclusion in the information society. Those who are most susceptible to being marginalized in society are at the highest risk of being left behind in IT. The late adopters include the elderly, people with disabilities, people in low-skilled low-pay employment, members of ethnic minority groups, and those who are dependent on state benefits. Often these groups also lack access to equipment, as well as the necessary competence and the confidence. The absence of ICT competence compounds existing levels of social exclusion.

Characteristics of early adopters	Characteristics of late adopters
Young	Older
Urban	Rural/deprived urban
Employed	Outside workforce (for example, housewives)
Professional	Non-professional (for example, farmers, manual workers)
High income	Lower income
High educational attainment	Lower educational attainment

(Information Society Commission, 2000b)

Developing universal IT skills is one of the greatest challenges faced by educators, similar to the challenge of universal literacy in the developed world a century ago. In her article 'Digital Divide or Digital Difference?' (2000), Ursula Howard has argued that there are five key issues for educators and government if the digital have-nots are to join the digital haves:

▌ access;
▌ basic skills;
▌ content;
▌ community; and
▌ pedagogy.

The problems of access are often associated with the cost of IT, and particularly the costs of going online. This is less of a problem in the United States, where local telephone calls are unmetered. It is important to provide as much public access as possible and to help people to overcome their fears of technology. And it is equally important to convince those people who are not online of the importance of becoming connected. It may be that, in the medium term, Internet TV together with cheap phone charges will be the best route towards a digitally inclusive society. The digital divide may not be bridged until every home and every workplace is connected to affordable information services.

People will be stimulated to join the digital revolution only if they are offered interesting and acceptable content, and materials that are accessible and acceptable to learners. This is a particular issue with minority groups who, for religious or cultural reasons, may have a problem with the Western (particularly US) dominance of the Internet. There is also an issue of community when it comes to bridging the digital divide. Digital TV will provide an additional source of access, but will this help, say, children wanting to do homework if adults want to watch TV programmes? Or will teenagers want to surf the Internet in view of their parents? There is therefore a short-term need for accessible training and hands-on facilities, particularly for those groups who have low Internet usage or who need to develop their computing skills. Conveniently situated learning hubs, computers in libraries and youth centres, after-school computer clubs, adult education Internet classes, community use of school computers, Internet cafés and in-company learning centres are all part of the answer.

However, the greatest challenge in bridging the digital divide is ensuring exciting and challenging pedagogy and building on the potential of the digital world. This is important because learning needs to build and exploit the hugely motivating force of computing, and channel it into demanding and useful directions. It does allow for new ways of learning, for example, greater opportunities for independent and learner-centred learning and more emphasis on personal research.

In a similar vein, Professor Nicholas Negroponte, of MIT's Media Laboratory in Boston, has recognized that the digital revolution has still failed to touch the lives of a great many people. In 2001, he established a new research consortium, together with the Centre for International Development at Harvard, called 'Digital Nations'. The approach is not to impose solutions, but rather to empower people in all walks of life to invent their own solutions. Creating a digitally inclusive society is the first step in managing knowledge. All organizations, whether public or private, need to recognize the waste that occurs from not empowering their most precious resource.

The following measures can bring about digital inclusiveness:

- the Internet in every home;
- digital TV with Internet link;
- low-priced telephone Internet links;
- making the internet relevant to the work of staff;
- enhanced access to ICT for learning;
- convenient local learning centres;
- ensuring that education stimulates the demand for knowledge;
- investment in computing in education;
- developing a relevant digital pedagogy.

Carly Fiorina, President and CEO of Hewlett Packard, sees the new technologies unlocking the people's richest core assets – their imagination and invention – in ways that could not have been foreseen even a few years ago, and allowing them to be used, regardless of place or culture. In her speech at the October 2000 Seattle conference, Ms Fiorina said, 'We are now at the beginning of a second renaissance, the Digital Renaissance. Invention is once again the prime virtue. But this time the tools for invention can be extended to every corner of the earth.'

Bridging the digital divide and creating a world that is digitally inclusive is a major challenge, some would say *the* major challenge, facing education. Imagination and determination are vital if the digital divide is to be turned into the digital dividend. Individuals and organizations need to be developed digitally, so that they can use technology to improve their life. Most importantly, education must ensure that it is relevant to the life of ordinary people, and stimulates the demand for lifelong learning. Unlocking talent and initiative can lead to a more inclusive society.

7 Knowledge-management gurus

'The Greeks said that to marvel is the beginning of knowledge and when we cease to marvel we will be in danger of ceasing to know.'

E. H. Gombrich (1993)

Knowledge management is a new discipline, with roots in a number of other disciplines, including management, information systems, business theory, social psychology and organizational behaviour. It has yet to develop a coherent set of theories, but some clear themes and lines of thought have emerged.

As in all disciplines, a number of important thinkers are influencing the development and direction of knowledge management. While there is no agreed list of knowledge-management 'greats', there are certain writers who have been particularly influential. Management theorists such as Peter Drucker and Chris Argyris have made significant contributions to the way we think about the issues of the knowledge age. Peter Senge has shown the importance of learning organizations to the success of any knowledge-creation venture, while Drucker has also shown how information and knowledge have become an important, if not *the* most important, organizational resource. Dorothy Leonard has demonstrated how innovation is essential to ensure that core knowledge capabilities do not turn into core rigidities. Nonaka and Takeuchi have made important contributions to theories on the nature of knowledge, emphasizing the importance of tacit knowledge to competitive advantage. On a similar theme, Thomas H. Davenport has argued that knowledge management should be seen as more than information process management, but should be a part of the integral workings within each organization.

Chris Argyris

Chris Argyris is James Bryant Constant Professor Emeritus of Education and Organizational Behaviour at Harvard University. A psychologist by training, he is one of the most influential management theorists of his generation. His list of publications over four decades is prestigious and includes *Organizational Learning: A theory of action perspective*, written with Donald Schon (1978); *Knowledge for Action: A guide to overcoming barriers to organizational change* (1993); and *On Organizational Learning* (1993).

One of Argyris's main themes is that organizations need to become learning organizations. He first used the phrase in *Organizational Learning*, where he argued that organizations fail when their culture inhibits learning. He explained it by using his famous Model I and Model II theories, contrasting two different organizational models – one effectively inhibits learning, while the other encourages it. Model I organizations operate institutional self-censorship. Managers who operate in a Model I setting are defensive, striving to retain complete control and to impose their will on others. As a result, they inhibit the interplay of genuine and honest communication between organizational members, who have to limit themselves to expressing ideas that are appropriate to the maintenance of the existing institutional culture. In Model I organizations, people avoid confrontation and argument. The organization only receives knowledge that its managers want to hear and messages are predominantly commentary. The only learning that takes place – what Argyris calls *single loop learning* – is how to conform. The result is that management is self-sealing and becomes removed from reality and the organization can get itself into serious trouble without understanding why. Not suprisingly, Model I organizations do not deal effectively with knowledge issues.

At the heart of the Model I organization's problems is the knowledge gap. Argyris sums this up as the difference between *theories espoused* and *theories in use.* This is about honesty. 'Theories espoused' are dialogues in which people talk about honesty, but the culture prevents honesty. One of his prime examples is the Soviet Union, where the reality was at variance with the espoused ideology of the regime. Its collapse came about because it could not face up to the realities of the world.

In contrast, Model II organizations are those that employ the concept of 'theories in use', with honest communication and discussion taking place. Model II organizations are those in which real learning takes place. Argyris argues that real learning takes place not when an organization refines its knowledge (single loop learning), but when it engages in *double loop learning*, which takes place when theories are overturned, updated and replaced.

A Model II organization uses genuine self-criticism and has a capacity for honest self-assessment. To do this effectively, managers often require training to help them reduce their defensiveness and to deal effectively with diverse opinions. This will enable them to use constructive reasoning, leading to genuine and effective organizational learning and change. Clearly, there are important implications here for educational institutions and the ideas need no translation for educational managers. They are as directly applicable to a school or university as to a corporate setting.

Thomas H. Davenport and Laurence Prusak

Thomas H. Davenport is Professor of Management Information Systems at Boston University School of Management, and Director of the Andersen Consulting Institute for Strategic Change. Prior to this he was a Professor of Information Management at the University of Texas, Austin, and has engaged in research for Ernst & Young, McKinsey and the CSC Index. This varied experience has given him some important insights into the knowledge-management process and this has made his writings particularly influential.

Laurence Prusak is Managing Principal with the IBM Consulting Group in Boston and is the group's worldwide competency leader for knowledge. Before joining IBM he had worked for Ernst & Young's Centre for Business Innovation.

Thomas Davenport and Laurence Prusak have written and co-authored a number of important books, including *Process Innovation: Re-engineering work through information technology* (Davenport, 1993); *Knowledge in Organizations* (Prusak, 1997); *Information Ecology: Mastering the information and knowledge environments* (co-authored, 1997); *Working Knowledge: How organizations manage what they know* (co-authored, 1998).

Davenport and Prusak have drawn upon their consulting experience to understand how organizations can manage their intellectual assets and turn corporate wisdom into market value. Their main thesis is that, without knowledge, an organization cannot effectively organize itself. Knowledge enables it to function. However, in their view, that knowledge does not have to be newly created. It only needs to be new to the organization; it can be bought in or hired, as well as generated internally.

Some of the basic principles of their work appear in Davenport's 10 principles of knowledge management:

1. Knowledge management is expensive (but so is stupidity!).
2. Effective management of knowledge requires hybrid solutions of people and technology.

3. Knowledge management is highly political.
4. Knowledge management requires knowledge managers.
5. Knowledge management benefits more from maps than models, more from markets than from hierarchies.
6. Sharing and using knowledge are often unnatural acts.
7. Knowledge management means improving knowledge work processes.
8. Knowledge access is only the beginning.
9. Knowledge management never ends.
10. Knowledge management requires a knowledge contract.

Davenport argues that in the early stages of knowledge management, organizations managed their knowledge assets in the same way that they managed their physical assets. That is to say, they worked on capturing and recording information so that it could be easily accessed in a *knowledge warehouse*. This allowed knowledge to be created and shared throughout the organization, as and when required. While this may seem to make sense, it does bring about a paradox that has particular implications in the knowledge age – it requires knowledge workers being 'told' how to do their job. Yet autonomy is one of the key attributes of the knowledge worker. In order to address this issue it is important to give knowledge workers ownership of the design of the new processes. In addition, knowledge managers need to spend their time with knowledge workers in order to have a greater insight into the same processes.

Interestingly, Davenport argues that knowledge management, as it develops as a discipline, draws in a number of related management subjects – from organizational learning and e-learning, through to business intelligence. He also argues that this multi-disciplinary focus may lead to a loss of focus and concentration, and a resultant loss of momentum. It is possible to forget what knowledge management can teach us, but it can be useful to draw on closely (or even distantly) related topics. The common objective of using knowledge to achieve organizational goals means that knowledge management may be an appropriate 'umbrella' term that embraces a wide range of topics, subjects and ideas.

In 1998, Tom Davenport and Laurence Prusak published *Working Knowledge*, subtitled *How organizations manage what they know*. In it, they drew an important distinction between data, information and knowledge. They made the point that knowledge is 'broader, deeper and richer than data or information'; knowledge is experience, 'ground truth', complexity, rules of thumb, intuition, values and beliefs. They also offered the following definition of knowledge:

Knowledge is a fluid mix of framed experiences, values, contextual information, and expert insight that provides a framework for evaluating and incorporating new experiences and information. It originates and is applied in the minds of knowers. In organizations, it often becomes embedded not only in documents or repositories but also in organizational routines, processes, practices and norms. (1998)

What does this mean for educational organizations? In some ways, the emphasis on organizational culture rather than business processes, found in Davenport's writings, makes knowledge management ideally suited for educational contexts. The management of educational knowledge workers, within a school, college or university setting, has always demanded a balance between autonomy and direction. Indeed, much work in the field of education has attempted to understand some of the processes that lead to particular cultures. In part, a particular cultural form depends upon the adoption of certain forms of leadership and teamworking styles. Telling or sharing styles of management can lead to cultures that are highly individualized or have a potential for collaborative working. Davenport and Prusak's focus on the autonomy direction paradox gets to the very heart of knowledge management in educational settings and presents educational managers with some important messages to ponder.

Peter Drucker

Peter F. Drucker was born in Austria in 1909 and educated in Austria, Germany and England. From 1929, he worked in England as a journalist and advisor to an international bank. In 1937, he moved to the United States, where he worked as an adviser to a number of British banks and as a newspaper correspondent for several British newspapers. Later, he was employed as a management consultant. A naturalized American citizen, Drucker was a professor of management at New York University from 1950 to 1972 and, since 1971, has been Clarke Professor of Social Sciences at the Claremont Graduate University in Claremont. He is honorary chairman of the Drucker Foundation.

Peter Drucker is one of the most important management writers of the last century and his writings cover a very broad spectrum of topics and ideas. He is the author of 31 books, including *Technology, Management and Society* (1970); *Post-Capitalist Society* (1993); and *Management Challenges for the 21st Century* (1999).

In his writings, Drucker argues that the most important things that management needs is to learn how to manage knowledge workers, as they are the most valuable assets of a 21st-century organization. He makes the point that six major factors determine the productivity of knowledge workers:

1. The productivity of knowledge workers demands the question, 'What is the task?'.
2. Responsibility for their productivity needs to be placed on the individual knowledge workers themselves. They have to manage themselves. They have to have *autonomy*.
3. Continuing innovation has to be part of the work, task and responsibility of knowledge workers.
4. Knowledge work requires continuous learning on the part of the knowledge worker, and continuous teaching on part of the knowledge worker organization.
5. Productivity of the knowledge worker is not, at least not primarily, a matter of the quantity of the output. Quality is at least as important.
6. Finally, knowledge-worker productivity requires the knowledge worker to be seen and treated as an 'asset' rather than a 'cost'. Knowledge workers have to want to work for an organization in preference to all other opportunities.

The value in a knowledge company resides in the know-how of each employee, more than in the fixed assets on the production line. According to Drucker, '. . . it is certain that the emergence of the knowledge worker and of the knowledge worker's productivity as key questions will, within a very few decades, bring about fundamental changes in the structure and nature of the economic system'.

One of Drucker's main arguments is that the effective organization puts individuals in jobs where they can have the most impact. In other words, an individual is put in a role, and then allowed to develop that role in order to maximize his or her strengths. He argues that the shift to the knowledge age provides organizations with four ways to develop and motivate knowledge workers:

1. Know people's strengths.
2. Place them where they can make the greatest contribution.
3. Treat them as associates.
4. Expose them to challenges.

Knowledge workers are more concerned with being effective rather than counting the hours of the working week. Knowledge workers need to believe in their work and be proud of the contribution they are making.

Drucker argues that smart organizations understand this. Interestingly, he points out that the best way to develop people is to provide them with opportunities to participate as volunteers in non-profit organizations. Being a volunteer requires a belief in the organization's mission. Volunteering provides individuals with responsibility, and the opportunity to see results, and to learn about their strengths, weaknesses and their own values.

Drucker's work is very important for education and three elements stand out. First, the vast majority of teachers, lecturers and researchers are recruited into education to teach rather than to manage or administrate. Educational organizations should play to their strengths, and the beliefs and values that brought them into education in the first instance. Managerial solutions that conflict with their values as educators should not be imposed on them. They should not be given so much accountability-based paperwork that they cannot exercise their art properly as educators. Second, and quite paradoxically, the knowledge age requires a revisiting of 'older values' in the management of educational professionals. There needs to be a re-emphasis on 'vocation' and this leads to the third element, which is that it is important to give educational professionals the autonomy to get the job done, within a robust sense of values. By definition, teachers are knowledge workers and if they are doing their job properly they require only light-touch management.

Dorothy Leonard

Dorothy Leonard, best known as the author of *Wellsprings of Knowledge* (1995), is William J. Abernathy Professor of Business Administration at the Harvard Business School. Professor Leonard joined the Harvard faculty in 1983 after teaching at the Sloan School of Management at Massachusetts Institute of Technology. Her research and consulting interests are in organizational innovation, new technology commercialization, and the generation, identification and management of knowledge assets in companies. In addition, she has conducted research in the areas of creating and exploiting knowledge-based assets, the power of tacit knowledge, and the methods of enhancing group creativity. Her other books include *When Sparks Fly* (with Walter Swap, 1999).

In *Wellsprings of Knowledge*, Leonard discusses the managerial activities that maintain innovation and develop strategic technological capabilities. She argues that core capabilities are the starting point for managing organizational knowledge. They are built up over time and are difficult to replicate, and constitute the competitive advantage of the firm. However, they are only core if they embody proprietary knowledge, which is not available from public sources. If it is to build and create core capabilities, an organization must know how to manage it, but it must also possess an understanding of what constitutes a core capability.

However, Leonard identifies a perplexing paradox in managing core capabilities. Its strength is also simultaneously its weakness. Capabilities can turn into rigidities. Once a success becomes a success, there is a tendency not to question it and, therefore, not to recognize the fact when an activity or a process moves into obsolesce or becomes less applicable in a different situation. In order to avoid the development of core rigidities, the organization has to engage in some of the following knowledge-building activities:

- the development of shared, creative problem-solving skills;
- implementing and integrating new technologies;
- formal and informal experimentation;
- the importation of expertise from outside the firm.

Organizations that engage in these activities become self-regenerating. Leonard argues that some of the key characteristics of organizations that continuously renew themselves are:

- an enthusiasm for knowledge;
- a drive to stay ahead in knowledge;
- the tight coupling of complementary skill sets;
- iteration in activities;
- higher-order learning;
- leaders who listen and learn.

Leonard's analysis has a number of important implications for educational organizations. First, the importance of what she calls 'firm-specific skills', or tacit knowledge, indicates why it is difficult to replicate the performance of a successful organization. She argues that innovations cannot simply be imported from one organization to another; school- or college-specific expertise cannot be imported easily, because outsiders take time to understand the culture. Educational organizations need to focus on developing the organizational-specific knowledge of its members; talent needs to be home-grown.

Second, creative problem-solving requires the recruitment of people with different ideas, in order to extend the range and to prevent any reliance on existing or familiar solutions. Third, schools and other educational organizations need to work extremely hard to ensure that they are connected to the outside world, in order to tap into the tacit knowledge of external stakeholders. Fourth, the pool of knowledge within a school or educational organization is not static and requires constant replenishment. The development of knowledge-creation capabilities is fundamental.

Ikujiro Nonaka

Ikujiro Nonaka received his BA in Political Science in 1958 from Waseda University, and a PhD in Business Administration from University of California, Berkeley. He was Professor at the Faculty of Management, Nanzan University, from 1977 to 1979. He is a professor of the Graduate School of International Strategy at Hitotsubashi University and the Xerox Distinguished Professor in Knowledge at the Haas School of Business, University of California, Berkeley. Some of his key work can be found in *The Knowledge-Creating Company* (1995, written jointly with Hirotaka Takeuchi) and *Enabling Knowledge Creation* (2000, co-authored with George von Krogh and Kazuo Ichijo).

In *The Knowledge-Creating Company*, Nonaka lays out a model of how knowledge is created through the interaction between explicit and tacit knowledge. He and his co-author identify four major processes of knowledge conversion:

1. Socialization – a process of converging new tacit knowledge through shared experiences.
2. Externalization – a process of articulating tacit knowledge through dialogue and reflection.
3. Combination – a process of converging explicit knowledge into more complex and systematic sets of explicit knowledge.
4. Internalization – a process of embodying explicit knowledge into tacit knowledge.

When these four processes interact, the organization can then enjoy what can be described as a knowledge-creation spiral. However, a limitation of the work in *The Knowledge-Creating Company* is that it focused on the process of knowledge creation rather providing practical guidance as to how to go about it. In *Enabling Knowledge Creation*, five knowledge-enablers are described:

1. Instil a knowledge vision – this legitimizes knowledge-creation activities across the organization.
2. Manage conversations – the creation of conditions of trust which allow creativity, the sharing of tacit knowledge and concept creation.

3. Mobilize knowledge activists – this emphasizes the people who trigger and coordinate knowledge-creation processes.
4. Create the right context – the development of the organization's structure, project teams, finding space for the creation of knowledge.
5. Globalize local knowledge – the dissemination of the information across many levels of the organization.

This approach emphasizes the social nature of knowledge creation. Nonaka and his fellow authors recognize that attempts to manage knowledge creation are likely to fail, especially if there is a reliance on technology or systems, as opposed to strong cultures of learning and sharing. The key insight is that the creation of knowledge is difficult to control or manage, and it may be inherently uncontrollable.

Interestingly, in respect of educational organizations, Nonaka and his fellow authors emphasize that the key requirement for a knowledge worker is his or her *humanness*, rather than professional qualifications or formal status. Restricting the idea of knowledge creation only to teachers or headteachers inhibits the ability of the educational institution to unleash the full potential of its entire staff. Administrators, receptionists, estate managers and cleaners all have a role to play in knowledge creation. They may well find new and novel ways to develop the mission or vision of the institution through their interaction with students and other stakeholders.

Peter Senge

Professor Peter M. Senge is Director of the Organizational Learning Center at the Massachusetts Institute of Technology's Sloan School of Management. He is also Chairperson of the Society for Organizational Learning (SoL). This is a worldwide community of organizations, academics and consultants dedicated to the 'interdependent development of people and their institutions'. Senge received a BS in engineering from Stanford University, an MS in social systems modelling and his PhD in management from MIT. His best-selling books include *The Fifth Discipline: The art and practice of the learning organization* (1990); *The Fifth Discipline Fieldbook: Strategies and tools for building a learning organization* (1994); *The Dance of Change: The challenges to sustaining momentum in learning organizations* (1999); *Schools that Learn* (2000).

Organizational learning took an important step forward with the publication of *The Fifth Discipline*, and Senge was propelled to prominence. He was advocating the notion of the company as a learning organization, articulating five disciplines of the learning organization and emphasizing that most organizations suffer from several deficiencies in their learning. In his view, organizations can suffer from a functional myopia. Generally, the better-educated a person or a workforce, the better they are at being defensive or blocking open communication. This is linked to a fear of change and a lack of a culture of experimentation. Fear means that no one looks at the benefits that learning can bring. Managers fail to see the big picture and do not see the connective links when taking decisions or introducing strategy.

Senge identifies a number of core disciplines for building a learning organization and overcoming these learning deficiencies:

▌ Systems thinking – the recognition that business and human endeavours are systems held together by invisible interrelated actions. Systems thinking helps people to see the big picture and enables them to see the interrelationships between the parts. The discipline of systems thinking is all about widening and deepening knowledge and can lead to new insights.

▌ Personal mastery – self-knowledge, or the process of continually refining and developing a personal vision and focusing energies and commitment. It can lead to a greater understanding of personal goals and values.

▌ Mental models – the deeply ingrained assumptions, generalizations or images that influence how someone understands the world. Tacit knowledge is held in personal cognitive maps. According to Senge, this is the most difficult discipline but has the greatest potential leverage.

▌ Building shared vision – the development of knowledge through the sharing of ideas and thinking. The process of building a collective vision through dialogue and discussion and assisting in the process of moving personal mastery into team knowledge.

▌ Team learning – this involves dialogue and team members suspending assumptions and entering into genuine thinking together. It makes tacit knowledge explicit and vice versa, develops collective understanding, and helps people to understand each other.

In *Schools that Learn* (2000), Senge reflects upon the experiences over the past five to ten years of applying the theories, tools and methods of organizational learning to schools. The book is based on the work of hundreds of teachers, administrators, parents, community leaders and students. It aims to capture the insights and challenges of an emerging field, and to make them available in a manner that will help others engaged in similar work. As such, it is very relevant for educators.

Some of the key implications of Senge's work for educators are as follows:

▌ Schools, colleges and universities cannot be in a state of permanent excellence. As they practise the disciplines of the learning organization, they either become better or worse.

▌ Copying the best practices of others may do more harm than good; it is important for educators to find their own way. This is an interesting challenge to the benchmarking debate that has dominated the thinking about achieving educational excellence.

▌ Through the application of systems thinking and the changing of mental models, educators are able to create their own reality, rather than being 'stuck' with a particular type of school, for example, because of the nature of the pupil population.

▌ Educational organizations are dynamically complex; the relationship between cause and effect is subtle, and the effects of actions are not immediately obvious.

8 The knowledge-management checklist

'How do we know what we know?'

E. Sallis (2001)

Knowledge management presents an interesting dilemma. Can knowledge really be managed? Knowledge is a largely cognitive and very personal process, while management is at the heart of the organizational process. Today's knowledge workers find it increasingly difficult to be managed in the traditional sense. This leaves organizations with an interesting set of problems.

The only way to reconcile knowledge and management, and to enable an organization to harness its key resource successfully, is to ensure that the organizational culture contains the right elements and processes. The knowledge-management self-assessment checklist is designed to assist in the process of developing an effective culture. It can help an institution to see where it is in relationship to the main indicators of knowledge-management success.

Other self-assessment and benchmarking tools include the KNOW Network (at www.knowledgebusiness.com). This is a Web-based knowledge community dedicated to sharing best practice, leading to superior organizational performance. The 'Most-Admired Knowledge Enterprises' study is the established benchmark for knowledge-based organizations and can be used as a basis for organizational self-assessment. Since 1998, it has conducted the MAKE awards. One education institution, MIT, has been a finalist. In 2001, the winner was General Electric of the United States, followed by Hewlett Packard, Buckman Laboratories, the World Bank and Microsoft. The MAKE awards use eight knowledge performance dimensions as the assessment framework, which was developed by Teleos. The criteria are as follows:

■ Success in establishing an enterprise knowledge culture.
■ Top-management support for managing knowledge.
■ Ability to develop and deliver knowledge-based goods/services.
■ Success in maximizing the value of the enterprise's intellectual capital.
■ Effectiveness in creating an environment of knowledge sharing.
■ Success in establishing a culture of continuous learning.
■ Ability to manage knowledge to generate shareholder value.

Our own self-assessment criteria is somewhat different from that of the MAKE awards but it can be combined with theirs. It follows the themes in this book and concentrates on the strategic and leadership factors that are so crucial for successful knowledge management. For the purposes of self-assessment we use a rating system of 1–5, where 1 is high and 5 is low.

Self-assessment

Vision and mission

The organization:

	1	2	3	4	5

■ has a strong vision as a knowledge-based organization
■ has shared its vision with its stakeholders
■ has a mission to be a knowledge creator and a learning organization
■ can translate vision and mission into practical strategies

Strategy

The organization:

■ has modelled scenarios for its future
■ incorporates knowledge management into its overall strategy
■ has developed knowledge-management strategies
■ has organizational knowledge-sharing strategies
■ has strategies for exploiting its knowledge

Organizational culture

The organization:

	1	2	3	4	5

■ creates a culture that supports innovation, learning and knowledge sharing

■ puts knowledge and learning at the centre of its mission

■ has been successful in establishing a knowledge-sharing culture

■ has been successful in establishing a knowledge-creation culture

■ needs to understand that knowledge management is essential to organizational success

■ recognizes that knowledge management is a key organizational competence

Intellectual capital

The organization:

■ recognizes the value of its intellectual assets

■ places a book value on its knowledge

■ seeks to codify its tacit knowledge

■ seeks to value its intellectual assets

Learning organization

The organization:

■ creates a culture of continuous learning

■ defines the skills and competency necessary to create new knowledge

■ recognizes that emotional intelligence and its development are essential to knowledge creation

■ is creating its own corporate university

■ ensures that its staff can be creative and think 'out of the box'

■ has a strong middle-management development programme

■ uses action learning as a means of personal and team development

Leadership and management

The organization:

	1	2	3	4	5

▌ has senior-management support for managing knowledge

▌ recognizes the ambiguities and challenges in building communities of practice

▌ has a chief knowledge officer or a knowledge leader in place

▌ has developed a strategy for developing its middle managers

▌ has managers with the appropriate leadership styles for generating knowledge sharing

▌ has managers with the necessary competences to develop knowledge creation

Teamwork and learning communities

The organization:

▌ has a policy of encouraging the development of learning communities

▌ recognizes the need for intellectual autonomy by knowledge workers

▌ creates knowledge teams, using people from all disciplines

▌ recognizes that trust is central to its development of knowledge sharing

Sharing knowledge

The organization:

▌ has a process for sharing and collecting information

▌ has storytelling and learning histories processes in place

▌ has a process for recording critical incidents in the life of the organization

■ has a process for understanding how its competitors manage knowledge

■ has systems in place to allow everybody to find out what they need to know

Knowledge creation

The organization:

■ recognizes the sources of its new knowledge

■ has identified those people known to be 'experts' and shares that information

■ can turn new knowledge into products and services that add value to clients and customers

Digital sophistication

The organization:

■ has a clear vision and technological architecture

■ has ensured that there is no digital divide among its employees

■ has technologies in place that allow it to be knowledge-enabled

■ has collaborative technologies in place, including an intranet that allows for knowledge sharing to move to sophisticated GroupWare

■ allows employees to build virtual learning communities

Further reading

6, Perri and Jupp, Ben (2001) *Divided by Information? The 'digital divide' and the implications of the new meritocracy*, Demos, London

Allee, Verna (1997) *The Knowledge Evolution: Expanding organizational intelligence*, Butterworth-Heinemann, London

Arbnor, Ingeman and Bjerke, Björn (1997) *Methodology for Creating Business Knowledge*, 2nd edn, Sage Publications, London

Argyris, Chris and Schon, D (1978) *Organizational Learning: A theory of action perspective*, Addison-Wesley, Reading, MA

Argyris, Chris (1993) *Knowledge for Action: A guide to overcoming barriers to organizational change*, Jossey-Bass, San Francisco, CA

Argyris, Chris (1993) *On Organizational Learning*, Blackwell, Cambridge, MA

Brown, John Seely and Duguid, Paul (2000) *The Social Life of Information*, Harvard Business School Press, Boston, MA

Burgoyne, John, 'The Learning Organisation', *People Management*, 3 June 1999, Chartered Institute of Personnel and Development

Caseley, Clive, ed (2000) *Learning 2010*, Learning and Skills Development Agency, London

Clarke, Thomas and Clegg, Stewart (1998) *Changing Paradigms: The transformation of management knowledge for the 21st century*, HarperCollins Business, London

Cortada, James W and Woods, John A (2000) *The Knowledge Management Yearbook 2000–2001*, Butterworth Heinemann, Boston, MA

Daft, R and Lengel, R (1998) *Fusion Leadership*, Berrett-Koehler, San Francisco, CA

Davenport, Thomas H (1998) *Some Principles of Knowledge Management*, Graduate School of Business, University of Texas at Austin (www.bus.utexas.edu/kman/kmprin.htm)

Davenport, Thomas H and Prusak, Laurence (1998) *Working Knowledge: How organizations manage what they know*, Harvard Business School Press, Boston, MA

Further reading

Davenport, Thomas H and Prusak, Laurence (1997) *Information Ecology: Mastering the information and knowledge environments*, Oxford University Press, Oxford

Davenport, Thomas H (1993) *Process Innovation: Reengineering work through information technology*, Harvard Business Press, Boston, MA

Davis, Stan and Meyer, Christopher (2000) *Future Wealth*, Harvard Business School Press, Boston, MA

De Bono, Edward (2000) *Six Thinking Hats*, Penguin Books, London

Department of Trade and Industry (2000) *Our Competitive Future: Building the Knowledge-Driven Economy*

Despres, Charles and Chauvel, Daniele, eds (2000) *Knowledge Horizons*, Butterworth Heinneman, Boston, MA

Drucker, Peter (1970) *Technology, Management and Society*, Pan, London

Drucker, Peter (1993) *Post-Capitalist Society*, Harper Business, New York

Drucker, Peter (1999) *Management Challenges for the 21st Century*, Harper-Collins, New York

Gardner, Howard (1983) *Frames of Mind: The theory of multiple intelligences*, Basic Books, New York

Gladstone, Bryan (2000) *From Know-How to Knowledge: The essential guide to understanding and implementing knowledge management*, Industrial Society, London

Goleman, Daniel (1995) *Emotional Intelligence*, Bantam Books, New York

Goleman, Daniel (2000) *Working with Emotional Intelligence*, Bantam Books, New York

Gombrich, EH (1993) *Art and Illusion: Study in the psychology of pictorial representation*, Phaidon, London

Hamel, Gary and Prahalad, CK (1996) *Competing for the Future*, Harvard Business School Press, Boston, MA

Hamel, Gary (2000) *Leading the Revolution*, Harvard Business School Press, Boston, MA

Howard, Ursula (2000) 'Digital Divide or Digital Difference?', in *Learning 2010*, ed Clive Caseley, Learning and Skills Development Agency, London

Information Society Commission (2000) 'Early and Late Adopters of New Technology: Research into general public attitudes towards information and communications technology', Stationery Office, Dublin

Information Society Commission (2000a) 'How the General Public is Adopting to the Information Society in Ireland', Stationery Office, Dublin

Information Society Commission (2000b) 'Information Society Ireland' (third report of Ireland's Information Society Commission), Stationery Office, Dublin

Institute of Directors and Computacenter (2000) *Managing Knowledge in the Digital Age*, Directors Publications Ltd, London

Introna, Lucas D (1997) *Management, Information and Power: A narrative of the involved manager*, Macmillan, Basingstoke

Kennedy, Helena (1997) 'Learning Works: Widening participation in further education', Further Education Funding Council, Coventry

'KM in Practice: Executive report of the second international CKO summit', Luttrellstown Castle, Dublin, Ireland, March 1999, TFPL Ltd

Kotter, John (1996) *Leading Change*, Harvard Business School Press, Boston, MA

Leatherwood, C (1999) 'Technological Futures: Gendered visions of learning', in *Post-Compulsory Education*, **4** (1)

Leonard, Dorothy (1995) *Wellsprings of Knowledge: Developing and Sustaining the source of Innovation*, Harvard Business School Press, Boston, Massachusetts

Leonard, Dorothy and Swap, Walter (1999) *When Sparks Fly*, Harvard Business School Press, Boston, MA

Liebowitz, Jay and Beckman, Tom (1998) *Knowledge Organization: What every manager should know*, St Lucie Press, Boca Raton, Florida

MacDonald, John (1999) *Understanding Knowledge Management*, Institute of Management, Hodder & Stoughton, London

Mayer, John D and Salovery, Peter (1997) *What is Emotional Intelligence?*, Basic Books, New York

Meister, Jeanne (1998) *Corporate Universities: Lessons in building a world-class workforce*, McGraw-Hill

Morton, Clive (1998) *Beyond World Class*, Macmillan Business, Basingstoke

Morton, Clive (2000) 'Learning for the Knowledge-Driven Economy', inaugural professorial lecture, Middlesex University

Mulgan, Geoff (1998) *Connexity: Responsibility, freedom, business and power in the new century*, Vintage, London

Myers, Paul S (1996) *Knowledge Management and Organizational Design*, Butterworth-Heinemann, Boston, MA

National Telecommunications and Information Administration (1999) 'Falling Through the Net: Defining the digital divide', US Department of Commerce

National Telecommunications and Information Administration (2000) 'Falling Through the Net: Towards digital inclusion', US Department of Commerce

Nonaka, Ikujiro (1991) 'The Knowledge-Creating Company', *Harvard Business Review*, November–December

Nonaka, Ikujiro and Takeuchi, Hirotaka (1995) *The Knowledge-Creating Company*, Oxford University Press, New York

Nonaka, Ikujiro, 'A Dynamic Theory of Organizational Knowledge Creation', *Organization Science*, **5** (1) February 1994

Nonaka, Ikujiro and Takeuchi, Hirotaka, 'Toward Middle Up-Down Management: Accelerating information creation', *Sloan Management Review* Spring 1998

Nonaka, Ikujiro, 'Creating Organizational Order out of Chaos: Self-renewal in Japanese firms', *California Management Review* Spring 1998

Nonaka, Ikujiro and Konno, N (1998) 'The Concept of Ba: Building a foundation for knowledge creation', *California Management Review*, **40** (3)

Nonaka, Ikujiro, Von Krogh, George and Ichijo, Kazuo (2000) *Enabling Knowledge Creation*, Oxford University Press, Oxford

OECD (2000) 'Learning to Bridge the Digital Divide', Organization of Economic Co-operation and Development, Paris

Polanyi, Michael (1966) *The Tacit Dimension*, Doubleday, New York

Polanyi, Michael (1973) *Personal Knowledge: Towards a post-critical philosophy*, Routledge & Kegan Paul, London

Prusak, Laurence, ed (1997) *Knowledge in Organizations*, Butterworth-Heinemann

Regans, RW (1998) *ABC of Action Learning*, Lemos & Crane, London

Rosenberg, Marc J (2001) *e-Learning Strategies for Delivering Knowledge in the Digital Age*, McGraw-Hill, New York

Ryle, Gilbert (1949) *The Concept of Mind*, Hutchinson, London

Sallis, Edward and Hingley, Peter (1992) *Total Quality Management*, Coombe Lodge Report, The Staff College, Bristol

Sallis, Edward (2002) *Total Quality Management in Education*, 3rd edn, Kogan Page, London

Salovey, Peter and Slayter, David J, eds (1997) *Emotional Development and Emotional Intelligence*, Basic Books, New York

Schools IT 2000 (1999–2000) 'Innovative ICT Projects in Irish Schools: A catalogue of projects supported by the schools integration project under Schools IT 2000', National Centre for Technology in Education, Dublin

Seltzer, Kimberly and Bentley, Tom (2001) *The Creative Age: Knowledge and skills for the new economy*, Demos, London

Senge, Peter M (1990) *The Fifth Discipline: The art and practice of the learning organization*, Century Business, London

Senge, Peter M (1994) *The Fifth Discipline Fieldbook: Strategies and tools for building a learning organization*, Nicholas Brealey Publishing, London

Senge, Peter M *et al* (1999) *The Dance of Change: The challenges to sustaining momentum in learning organizations*, Nicholas Brealey Publishing, London

Senge, Peter M *et al* (2000) *Schools That Learn*, Nicholas Brealey Publishing, London

Stone, Douglas, Patton, Bruce and Heen, Sheila (1999) *Difficult Conversations: How to discuss what matters most*, Penguin Books, New York

Tapscott, Don (1996) *The Digital Economy: Promise and peril in the age of networked intelligence*, McGraw-Hill, New York

Tapscott, Don (1998) *Growing Up Digital: The rise of the net generation*, McGraw-Hill, New York

Tissen, Rene, Andriessen, Daniel and Lekanne Deprez, Frank (2000) *The Knowledge Dividend: Creating high performance through value-based knowledge management*, Financial Times Prentice Hall, London

Wenger, Etienne (1998) *Communities of Practice*, Cambridge University Press, Cambridge

World Bank (1998/9) *Knowledge for Development*, World Bank

Index

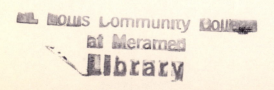